Railways
South East

The Album

Capital Transport

First published 1994

ISBN 185414 165 1

Published by Capital Transport Publishing
38 Long Elmes, Harrow Weald, Middlesex

Printed by Bath Midway Press
16-20 Midlands Industrial Estate
Holt, Wiltshire

**Welcome to Railways South East – The Album,
the first we hope of a number. To those who knew
us as a magazine, we hope you like the new format.**

**Some of the country's top names in railway writing
and photography have contributed to this book,
one of the last projects undertaken by Professor
H.P. (Pat) White before his death in February 1994.
His article on the Mid-Sussex line starts us off.**

**Articles based on original research are always
welcome for possible future use and should be
sent to the Harrow Weald address shown above.**

Enjoy the Album.

**Front Cover Ex-SECR P Class 0-6-0T No.1556, now preserved on the Kent & East Sussex
Railway, depicted as it might have appeared in the 1930s on that line near Wittersham
Road.** Oil Painting by Peter Green GRA

**Back Cover Continental travel almost a century ago. This pre-First World War poster, by
an unknown artist, encourages people to travel the LSWR route via Southampton and
Le Havre.** Courtesy Frank B. Smith

**Title Page A very unusual sight on Whit Monday, 18th May 1959, was that of a
Wainwright C Class 0-6-0 No.31683 on a down empty stock train near Bickley Junction,
the headcode indicating that it was for Dover, via Tonbridge. The SR's South Eastern
Division must have been in a parlous state for motive power that day for an 0-6-0 to
appear on main line empty stock.** R.C. Riley

**Opposite Following the formation of British Railways in January 1948 a start was soon
made to adorn locomotives to show the change. The lion and wheel image came later,
and at first various styles of 'British Railways' appeared on tender and tank sides,
generally applied when locomotives went for repair or overhaul. Renumbering of
locomotives to avoid duplication was also a gradual process, causing transitional
situations as seen at Waterloo. An IMS type 2.6.4T liveried as plain 'British Railways'
and carrying an IMS series number increased by the addition of a prefix 4, stands
alongside former Southern Railway 'Lord Nelson' 4.6.0 No.859 still wearing malachite
green, with 'Southern' on the tender. Soon it will be 30859. The presence of an IMS type
locomotive at Waterloo was an outcome of nationalisation.** Capital Transport collection

CONTENTS

Mid-Sussex to the South Coast

H.P. White

Above **The roundhouse of Horsham MPD in 1959.**
J. Scrace

The Mid-Sussex route came into being piecemeal and without an overall plan. It has since undergone varying fortunes. Electrified with high hopes, Dorking-Horsham is one of the South East's least used lines, while Three Bridges-Horsham enjoys an unprecedented service. The author traces a complex story.

The direct rail links from Brighton and Southampton to London were opened in 1841 and 1840 respectively. The only centre on the coast between them with any considerable traffic potential was Portsmouth. In 1847 the London Brighton and South Coast reached Portsmouth along the coast from Brighton and next year the London & South Western opened their line from Fareham on their even more circuitous 1841 route to Gosport and ferry.

The companies were satisfied with the status quo, which was more than the people of Portsmouth were, particularly as fares were based on the mileage of the roundabout routes. The LSWR, spurred on by fears that the South Eastern would take it over, themselves acquired the Portsmouth Direct line under construction to Havant via Haslemere and which would reduce their route by 21 miles. But this was in breach of an agreement with an infuriated LBSCR and led to the 'Battle of Havant' when the LSWR tried to run a goods train through in 1858. The matter was settled in Court and through running began the following January. Portsmouth was now 74½ miles from Waterloo, compared with the LBSCR's 95¼ miles via Brighton.

The latter now revived a scheme for a direct route initiated by the London & Croydon when promoting their West Croydon–Epsom Town line which opened in 1847. But the development of the route, usually known as the Mid-Sussex line, was most haphazard, without at first any overall plan or policy other than possibly trying to keep the LSWR out of west Sussex. And this led to a line which, constructed largely on the cheap, has resulted in anything but a high-speed and easily worked line.

Development of the Mid-Sussex line
South of Dorking lay the underdeveloped and sparsely-populated Weald, an area of forest and backward farming, with the small market town of Horsham and the ancient port of Arundel as virtually the only places of consequence. It was true the main line to Brighton ran through an equal traffic desert, but the prize of Brighton lay at the end.

Horsham was reached on 14th February 1848 by an 8½ mile branch from Three Bridges (its very name indicating it was then in the middle of nowhere) on the Brighton line. In 1856 the Epsom & Leatherhead was promoted to forestall a LSWR creation, the Wimbledon and Dorking, which posed a threat to Horsham. The E&L became joint property from Epsom Junction immediately north of the present Epsom station. The LBSCR began running trains over the 3¾ mile line on 8th August 1859.

Meanwhile, in 1857 the Mid-Sussex Railway was incorporated to build a line 17½ miles long from Horsham to Coultershaw Mill, allegedly near Petworth and where the station of that name was located. This was opened as a single line on 10th October 1859. Two gaps now remained, the first on the possible route alternative to that via Three Bridges, from Leatherhead to Horsham. This was closed by the independent Horsham, Dorking & Leatherhead incorporated in 1862 to link Horsham with a junction on the South Eastern's Redhill–Reading line east of Dorking (Deepdene) station. Powers for the remaining 4½ miles to Leatherhead were obtained by the LBSCR the next year and in 1864 they absorbed the smaller company. But slow progress was made and Dorking was not reached until 11th March 1867 and Horsham

Above **The LBSCR scene at Horsham. A fast train leaves for London via Three Bridges headed by a B2 4-4-0. The Southern converted the up platform and bays into an island.** Lens of Sutton

on 1st May, the spur to the SER being ready on the same day. Horsham is 37¼ miles from Victoria via Mitcham Junction and Dorking and 38 via Three Bridges.

The second gap was from the Mid-Sussex to the coast. Besides the question of a shorter route to Portsmouth, the LBSCR planned to develop the small general cargo port of Littlehampton as a packet port for Honfleur, St Malo and Jersey. In addition, seaside holidays were growing among the middle classes and Littlehampton and Bognor were benefiting. Accordingly in 1862 the LBSCR obtained powers for a line from Hardham Junction on the Mid-Sussex, three-quarters of a mile south of Pulborough, for nine miles to Arundel Junction on the Coast line. The line opened on 3rd August 1863. From 1863 the Three Bridges route was the only one, but when that via Dorking became available in 1867 the LBSCR made it the principal one.

The three Horsham stations –

The original one of 1848, the terminus of the branch from Three Bridges. RCHS–Spence collection

The 1859 station, built for the opening of the Mid-Sussex on an adjoining site. J. Scrace collection

The Southern version, the present 'Art Deco' structure rebuilt in connection with the 1938 electrification. H.P. White

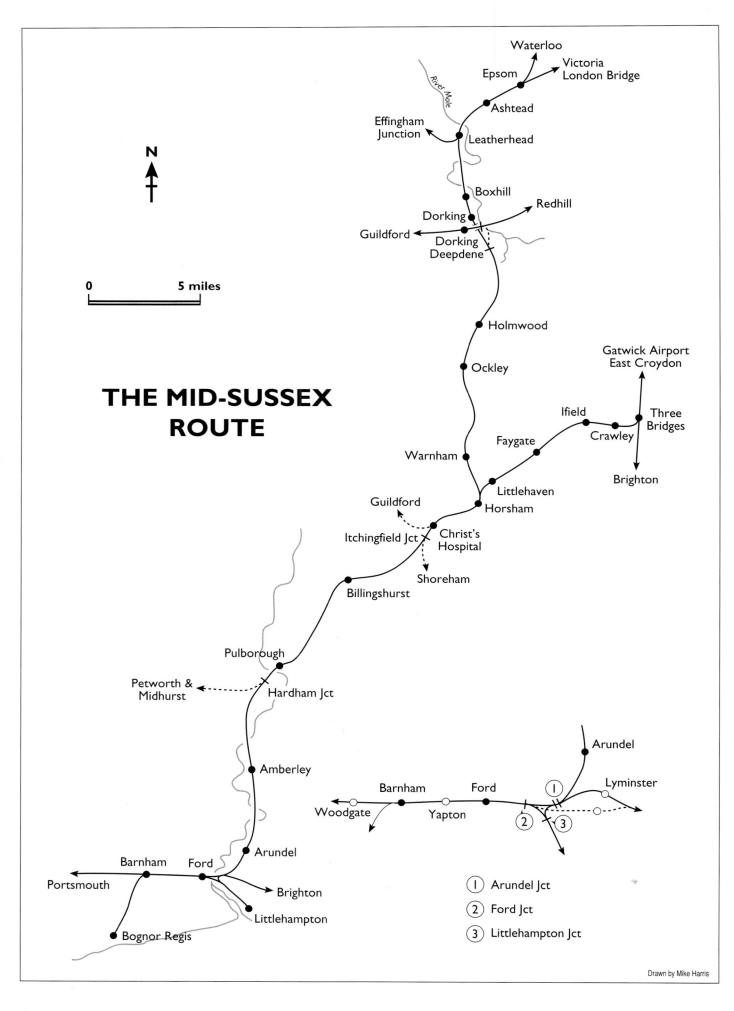

THE MID-SUSSEX ROUTE

N

0   5 miles

Waterloo

Victoria
London Bridge

Epsom

Ashtead

River Mole

Effingham
Junction

Leatherhead

Boxhill

Dorking

Redhill

Guildford

Dorking
Deepdene

Holmwood

Ockley

Gatwick Airport
East Croydon

Ifield

Three
Bridges

Faygate

Crawley

Warnham

Brighton

Littlehaven

Horsham

Guildford

Itchingfield Jct

Christ's
Hospital

Shoreham

Billingshurst

Pulborough

Petworth &
Midhurst

Hardham Jct

Amberley

Arundel

Barnham

Ford

Lyminster

Woodgate

Yapton

Arundel

Barnham

Ford

Portsmouth

Brighton

Littlehampton

Bognor Regis

① Arundel Jct

② Ford Jct

③ Littlehampton Jct

Drawn by Mike Harris

6

Description of the route

We may begin at Epsom, the Southern Railway's 1929 rebuild of the original joint station in the form of two island platforms. The ex-LBSCR line from Sutton, reached from both Victoria and London Bridge via West Croydon and via Mitcham Junction, joins the ex-LSWR's from Raynes Park by a severe curve. The first station, Ashtead, though an original one, was rebuilt in 1969. The first station at Leatherhead was a terminal one. But when the LSWR was extended to Effingham and the LBSCR to Horsham, each company provided a station south of the junction. Then in 1927 the Southern put in a connection to the south and the LSWR station closed. The LBSCR station, ornate and attractive, is a listed building.

The parallel west-east ridges of the North Downs and South Downs now lie athwart the route, but the situation is made much easier by the gaps created by the River Mole through the North Downs and the Arun gap through the South Downs. This led to consideration of using these and the Adur Gap in some of the early proposals for the route to Brighton. The physiography and the cost-cutting surface alignment means the Mid-Sussex lacks the major engineering features of the Brighton line.

But like all the Wealden lines, the scenery is attractive and the Mole Gap through the chalk Downs is the first such stretch. Mickleham Tunnel (524yds) cuts through a bend in the narrow valley and beyond is Boxhill and Westhumble (formerly 'and Burford Bridge'). On the insistence of the nearby landowner, elaborate station buildings in French chateau style were provided. Dorking (formerly Dorking North) lies at the south end of the gap. It now has an island platform on the down side and the LBSCR buildings by the same architect as Leatherhead and Boxhill have given way to a modern red brick office block, with the station offices on the ground floor. In effect Dorking has been the outer limit of a suburban service since electrification in 1925.

Beyond lies the Lower Greensand ridge, but this too has been pierced by the Mole and the only engineering feature is the moderate length of Betchworth tunnel (384yds) just beyond where the line passes under the Guildford–Redhill line. The 13½ miles to Horsham are through rolling wooded country with a pattern of small fields. Gradients are heavy and curves severe and frequent, which always mitigated against high speed. From Dorking there is a climb up to Holmwood, starting at 1 in 80 and culminating in 1.5 miles at 1 in 100. The descent to Warnham is even steeper, mainly at 1 in 90.

Although, as we shall see, the line has been thoroughly downgraded, it is still double and controlled by block posts at Holmwood (normally switched out) and Warnham, both equipped with semaphore signals, though there are intermediate colour lights north of Holmwood. Holmwood is now surrounded by new housing, but the other two are remote from the villages they serve, Ockley, which used to be Ockley and Capel, being midway between the two. They are unstaffed, though in recent years tickets were issued from the signal box at Warnham (until the signalmen refused to carry out this duty). At Holmwood the building on the overbridge was demolished in 1986, but at Ockley and Warnham rather dilapidated plain brick structures survive. The signal box at Warnham is maintained for the level crossing still with the traditional wooden gates.

The line from Three Bridges is much easier, following as it does the clay outcrop on which Gatwick Airport is built. It leaves the main line by a sharp curve immediately south of the station. The first and most important station is Crawley, at the centre of the Victorian part of the New Town, in which Three Bridges is now submerged. Like Dorking the station offices now occupy the ground floor of a large office block, the present station having been resited immediately to the east of the old one in 1968.

Ifield, promoted from halt status, now serves the western part of the New Town, Faygate, its buildings razed, is the only original stop other than Crawley. Littlehaven, another of the 1907 halts, is now well within the built-up area of Horsham.

The station at Horsham is the third on the site. The small and simple 1848 station was rebuilt for the opening of the Mid-Sussex in 1859 on an adjoining site. Its buildings were on the up side and an island platform on the down side. The Southern took the opportunity of the 1938 electrification to rebuild in its typical 'art deco' house style and to provide two island platforms. The loco depot was to the south of the typical Southern brick signal box and included a semi-roundhouse. There was a large goods yard on the west side, now partly used by the Civil Engineer, underlining the former importance of Horsham as a freight centre. South of the Three Bridges line is the recently closed petroleum terminal. All the signalling is colour light.

The line from here to Pulborough has a saw-tooth profile, with short sharp gradients mainly between 1 in 200 and 1 in 100, while curvature prevents fast speeds. It also provided problems for operating unfitted freight trains. Great care was needed to prevent 'snatching' at the frequent change of gradient and guards were instructed to keep their brakes partially applied.

The first station is Christ's Hospital, which dates from 1902 and was sited at Stammerham Junction, where the Guildford line diverged. Originally it also bore the title 'and West Horsham', having been provided to serve not only the eponymous public school, but also a railway-inspired housing project that never materalised. It was an enormous station, with seven platform faces serving five roads. There was a loop of the down main line and two lines served by three platforms before converging as the single-track Guildford branch (closed 1965). Since 1973 the whole elaborate structures have been reduced to two platforms and a small booking office rebuilt from the waiting room on the former platform 2. The formation of the Guildford line can be easily seen, but Itchingfield Junction (half a mile beyond) with the Shoreham line (closed 1966) has become very overgrown.

Billingshurst station, with its original tile-hung building on the up side, is now in the middle of the small town. It still retains its LBSCR signal box with mixed colour light and semaphores. It is six miles from Horsham and five miles beyond is Pulborough, again well sited in relation to the town. The buildings are on the down side and include the former goods shed alongside the platform. The up side was an island, the loop now removed, having been used by the Midhurst trains.

In the distance can be seen the line of the South Downs, with the gap created by the Arun, for which the line is making. Hardham Junction with the Midhurst branch, closed to passengers in 1955 and finally to freight in 1966, can be readily identified a mile to the south. Here the Arun Navigation passes under the line in tunnel but cannot be seen.

The line now crosses a flat marshy area before entering the Arun Gap at Amberley. The station has a simple brick building on the down side and is adjacent to the Chalk Pits Museum, its collection including industrial railway material. The 14-lever signal frame was installed by the Southern on the down platform in 1934 in replacement of the old box. Just to the south is the 83yd North Stoke tunnel. At the south end of the gap on the hilltop to the west is the stately pile of Arundel Castle and the very large Victorian Gothic RC Church. The station is about half a mile from the town, which covers the slope below the Castle. The station buildings on the up side are large, as is the usually well-filled car park, like those of Pulborough and Billingshurst. There was formerly a bay at the south end of the down platform, used until 1972 by Littlehampton shuttle trains.

Arundel is typical of the more important Mid-Sussex stations. J. Scrace

The Southern's 'Modern' style signal box controls the junction with the Coast Line 1¾ miles beyond. Immediately after is the triangular junction with the Littlehampton Branch, so there is through running from the Arundel as well as from the Brighton direction. This dates from 1887, when the Coast route was realigned to allow this. Previously all through traffic to Littlehampton had to reverse in Ford. The line now passes over the Arun by means of the 1938 fixed bridge which replaced the earlier opening one of 1887, which in turn superseded the original of 1846.

Immediately beyond is Ford station. The small cottage-like 1846 building is at the east end of the up platform. The down platform was an island until the recent removal of the loop line. The story of the Arundel stations is complex. In March 1846 the line from Worthing was opened to 'Littlehampton & Arundel' on the original formation near Lyminster. In June it was extended to Chichester and Ford was opened as 'Arundel'. The LBSCR built a road from

Arundel, which can be seen from the station at the far end of that road. The station at Lyminster became 'Littlehampton', but in 1850 it became 'Arundel and Littlehampton' and Ford got its name, probably because the LBSCR's road had fallen into disrepair. In 1863 Arundel got its new station (New Arundel for a time) as did Littlehampton, while the Lyminster facility closed (though a halt of that name opened in 1907). Paradoxically, though closed with the diversion, the original buildings remained.

Barnham (24¼ miles from Horsham) unlike the isolated Ford, is at the centre of an interwar development. It dates from the opening of the Bognor line. It was rebuilt in early Southern days from three to four platforms with two island platforms, but the loop on the north side has been removed and a more convenient entrance is being made, rather than the long subway to the booking office, which is somewhat remote from the station. The junction with the Bognor branch faces east.

The two-mile Littlehampton branch was opened in 1863, almost simultaneously with the line from Hardham Junction. It was doubled in 1887. That to Bognor (the Regis came when King George V had convalesced there in 1928), 3½ miles long, opened in 1864. The station on the Coast Line at Woodgate, opened as 'Bognor' in 1846, was then closed. Both the branches cross the flat coastal plain, but the terminal stations present a complete contrast. Both have four platforms in use controlled by impressive arrays of semaphore signals. Following fire damage, Bognor was rebuilt in 1902 with a large concourse and an extensive range of buildings which have become very dilapidated, and the station presents a very run down appearance as the site awaits development. On the other hand, Littlehampton, which had very poor facilities, was given a new building in 1987.

Above **The Arun Viaduct at Ford. On 4th August 1990 a Class 421 unit crosses on a westbound working.**
Brian Morrison

The development of the train services

Apart from that to Brighton, the LBSCR services were noted neither for frequency or speed. The same applied to the LSWR's services on the Portsmouth Direct via Guildford. The initial Mid-Sussex service in 1863 had five through trains from London — the fastest, the 16.00 from Victoria, reaching Portsmouth at 18.50. Local services were perhaps more lavish, the 1859 working timetable showing 12 weekday trains from Three Bridges to Horsham.

By 1889 there were six through trains, the 16.55 from London Bridge taking an even two hours to Portsmouth. The Dorking route was established as the main line, and in 1906 the five weekday semi-fasts from London to Portsmouth, all with connections to Little-hampton and Bognor, used that route. In addition the 07.58 'Parliamentary' from

London Bridge wandered down, calling vir-tually at all stations, while the 15.55 from Victoria went to Littlehampton. There were only two trains that would count as express, one for Isle of Wight passengers that ran fast from Victoria to Fratton and one that ran non-stop between Horsham and Chichester. As far as local services were concerned there were seven between Dorking and Horsham, 12 between Three Bridges and Horsham and seven between Horsham and Arundel. Local services were given a boost in 1907, when in connection with the new pull-and-push services, Ifield, Roffey Road (closed 1937) and Littlehaven Halts were opened.

At first the Southern made few basic changes, though by 1925 there were more through trains, especially from London Bridge in the evening peak, trains leaving at 17.00 for Littlehampton, 17.08 and 17.55 for

Bognor, the former with a Pullman Car. The 11.10 from London Bridge and 18.20 from Victoria ran via Three Bridges and the 09.00 also had a Pullman car.

Stock was virtually unchanged. The local services were still largely pull-and-push with 'Balloon' trailers hauled by the Stroudley D1 0-4-2Ts supplemented by the Billinton D3s. Ordinary local services were formed of mis-cellaneous ex-LBSC coaches and vans, for milk traffic handled in churns was still heavy. The main line trains were composed of ex-LBSCR coaches, the locomotives tending to be 'cascaded' from the Brighton line, the unsuccessful B2 4-4-0s and the ageing Gladstone 0-4-2s among them. The largest Brighton locos allowed were the B4x 4-4-0s and the Atlantics. After Grouping, LSWR 4-4-0s of the T9 and L12 classes were trans-ferred to these duties.

Electrification for suburban workings reached Dorking from Raynes Park in 1925 (1929 from London Bridge via Mitcham Junction) and Three Bridges in 1932. Thereafter the through semi-fasts continued to run, but local trains tended to be cut back to connect with electric services. The fundamental change came with electrification in 1938 of the whole Mid-Sussex. A lavish service was introduced based on an hourly semi-fast departure from Victoria, with Portsmouth and Bognor portions divided at Barnham (Littlehampton was reached via Haywards Heath and Worthing), and a half-hourly stopping service via Three Bridges which reached Bognor via Littlehampton and which provided connections into and out of the Coast Line trains. The new stock provided comprised 4-COR and 4-BUF units, the buffets furnished in highly contemporary art deco, and 2-BILS for the locals. Waterloo–Dorking services were extended hourly to Horsham and hourly to Holmwood, while the hourly service from London Bridge to Dorking was also extended to Horsham. There was also a half-hourly stopping service from Three Bridges, one train terminating at Littlehampton, the other going on to Bognor. The hourly fast trains from Victoria were routed for the most part via Dorking, a few via Three Bridges. At Barnham they were divided into Bognor and Portsmouth sections.

After the war, services were virtually restored to their pre-war levels. But in 1958 a drastic decline in the Dorking–Horsham local service began, the Holmwood trains going no further than Epsom. In 1967 the service became hourly, and two years later the off-peak trains ceased to call at the intermediate stations. From 1986 there were no off-peak trains beyond Dorking.

Similarly, south of Horsham experienced the same decline. First one, then the other of the half-hourly stopping services from Victoria via Three Bridges terminated at Horsham, while the 07 minutes past the hour 'semi-fast' from Victoria now stops at all stations from Horsham to Barnham. Until May 1993 there was a shuttle connection to Bognor off-peak. At peak periods Bognor portions were joined and split at Barnham. Littlehampton passengers had to change at Ford onto a Bognor–Littlehampton shuttle.

The growth of Crawley New Town, Gatwick Airport and East Croydon as traffic centres led to the diversion in 1978 of all the off-peak semi-fasts from the Dorking route to that via Three Bridges, the remainder following in 1984. This was not well received by Dorking passengers who were not only deprived of good southerly connections, but of fast, buffet services to London.

From October 1987 trains at about two-hourly intervals began to run again off-peak between Dorking and Horsham, calling only at Holmwood. Then from May 1991 an hourly shuttle service was put on, calling at all stations between Horsham and Dorking connecting at the latter with one of the Victoria services, while through trains at peak hours were provided. The shuttle was maintained by a two-car 416 unit with a crew of two.

In April 1992 the author made the round trip from Horsham by the 12.16 service. It conveyed two passengers, two more being picked up at Ockley. On the return there were again two passengers, one more boarding at Holmwood. Apparently this is not unusual; loadings at Dorking off-peak rarely exceed 6-10 and on 23rd April 1993 the

peak 17.57 from Victoria carried only 15 passengers south of Dorking. This must be the most sparsely utilised service over a comparable distance from London.

Freight services have never been important, and mainly of a local nature and inwards. Horsham was easily the most important destination, but there was a heavy brick traffic from Warnham until 1969 and milk was forwarded from the Express Dairy depot at Billingshurst. Christ's Hospital goods yard closed in 1961 and Ockley in 1962, all the others closing between 1964 and 1970, Horsham being the last to go, except for the oil traffic. There was some through traffic between the yards at Chichester and Norwood, including seasonal block trains of sugar beet for the East Anglian factories. But everything seems to have disappeared, the last victims being the occasional oil trains to the Horsham terminal which ceased in 1992. The port of Littlehampton thrives on landings of sea-dredged aggregates, but lost its rail connection many years ago.

The May 1993 timetables included some welcome improvements, the semi-fasts now conveying portions to and from Bognor throughout the day, eliminating the change at Barnham. In addition the Horsham–Dorking shuttle was replaced by an hourly through service, with peak extras, from Victoria to Horsham. Class 319 or 455 units are used for the workings via Dorking. Elsewhere all services are provided by Class 421 (4-CIG) and 423 (4-VEP) units employed apparently indiscriminately. It remains to be seen to what extent the improved services increase patronage, but at least a small start has been made. Meanwhile a trip over the Mid-Sussex is to be recommended for its scenic and operating interest.

The author wishes to express his grateful thanks to Alan A. Jackson for helpful comments and information freely given.

Holmwood station in 1969, the 17.02 Victoria–Horsham entering. The station building on the bridge has since been demolished. J. Scrace

Below **Vanishing freight.** With the oil terminal at Horsham scheduled for early closure, on 29th December 1992 Class 37/7 removes the empty tanks prior to running round and leaving for Ripple Lane with the 14.14 (WFO). Note the typical Southern signal box and the divergence of the Dorking (left) and Three Bridges (right) lines.
Brian Morrison

The Kemp Town Branch

R.C. Riley

The last scheduled passenger train, a Class D1 0-4-2T and pull and push trailer, rumbled into Kemp Town over 60 years ago on 31st December 1932, the day on which the last steam trains ran between London and Brighton prior to electrification. R.C. Riley tells the story of this short branch

Above **Stroudley 'Terrier' 0-6-0T No.B647 with a 'Balloon' trailer coach at Kemp Town station in July 1926.** H.C. Casserley

Facing Page Top **Kemp Town station interior, 23rd August 1952.** R.C. Riley

Facing Page Centre **Exterior view on the same date.** R.C. Riley

Facing Page Bottom **Lewes Road Viaduct in 1950. This has been demolished since closure of the branch.** R.C. Riley

Kemp Town takes its name from a one time Joint Lord of the Manor, Thomas Read Kemp, who built the architecturally fine estate there. It remains virtually unspoilt, one of the best examples of an estate conceived on the grand scale in the style of the Regency period. Many years elapsed before its success as a residential district was assured; the foundations of the estate were laid in 1823, but some houses remained untenanted until the mid 19th Century.

The London, Brighton & South Coast Railway obtained parliamentary authority to construct a branch to Kemp Town on 13th May 1864, at an estimated cost of £100,000, and the line opened to traffic on 2nd August 1869. A few days later a formal ceremony took place when the last brick was laid in the eastern pier of the central arch of Lewes Road viaduct. The privilege of carrying out this duty was accorded to Alderman Martin, to whom the contractors presented an elaborately engraved silver trowel which bore the inscription 'Presented to Mr Alderman Martin by the Contractors, Wm & Jno. Pickering, in commemoration of his turning the first sod of the Kemp Town Branch Railway on the 17th day of 1866, as Mayor of Brighton, and finished by him on the 6th day of August 1869.' Among speakers at this ceremony, Alderman Martin expressed hope that the line would prove advantageous to the east side of Brighton, which had been less

prosperous than the west. He also hoped that the railway company would provide a station near where they were standing as it was a rapidly expanding district in need of improved transport facilities.

Following this ceremony a banquet was held at The Old Ship Hotel. Reference was made in the speeches to the difficult time the railway was then going through. Apart from the 1866 collapse of the bankers Overend Gurney, there was the threat of a rival line leaving the LCDR line at Beckenham. In fact the bank collapse probably put paid to this but such lines as the Kemp Town branch could be regarded as a defence measure by the Brighton Company. Other speeches were made by LBSC Officers, notably J.P. Knight, Traffic Manager, and J.C. Craven, Locomotive Superintendent.

The earliest service over the branch consisted of nine trains each way on weekdays only, first, second and third class passengers being carried. The fare for the 2¼-mile journey from Brighton to Kemp Town was 6d (2.5p) first class and 2d third class with commensurate return fares. There were no intermediate stations and the journey took ten minutes. The first engine dedicated to the line's traffic was a Sharp Stewart 2-4-0T No.96 *Kemptown* of 1869, which surrendered its name to a new Stroudley 'Terrier' 0-6-0T No.64 five years later, the original engine then going to the Hayling Island branch.

The long awaited station at Lewes Road was opened on 1st September 1873; this had an island platform between up and down lines, with the main platform serving up trains only. Just west of the short Ditchling Road tunnel another intermediate station opened at London Road on 1st October 1877, for many years being used as the ticket collecting station for all westbound trains over the East Coast line. In 1876 powers were obtained for considerable developments at Kemp Town, where the company owned a large area. For some time excavations took place to remove the large amount of chalk from the site leading to the opening of a substantial goods and coal yard.

By this time Stroudley 'Terriers' provided the branch motive power, with an occasional Class D1 0-4-2T substituting to haul the five coach rake of Stroudley four-wheeled coaches. In the latter part of the 19th Century the weekday service consisted of 17 trains daily, while a Sunday service from 1879 was of seven trains. On 1st January 1906 a 48-seat petrol railcar was introduced with a half-hourly service of 32 trains daily and 24 on Sundays, 3rd Class only. This proved unreliable and D.E. Marsh, Locomotive Engineer from 1905, had devised a form of mechanical control enabling pull and push trains to be run. These consisted of a suitably fitted 'Terrier' with an open trailer of such dimensions as to make the engine look quite diminutive; these carriages gained the unofficial name of 'Balloons' and they survived in use until the early years of World War Two, when many of them became grounded for Home Guard use. L.B. Billinton, who succeeded Marsh in 1911, modified the pull and push apparatus to air control using the Westinghouse brake, a system subsequently adopted by the Southern Railway. During this period an additional halt platform was provided on the branch at Hartington Road on 1st January 1906. Since this was only 20 chains from Lewes Road it closed exactly five years later.

Although the service was now third class only there were business trains run, one in the morning and two in the evening on weekdays only, providing first class accommodation. These trains were worked by the Brighton Station Pilot and hence brought a larger engine to the branch. All services were withdrawn as a wartime economy measure on 1st January 1917 and passenger service was resumed on 10th August 1919, freight traffic on 2nd January 1922. This long interruption of train services and introduction of local bus

services proved disastrous and the weekdays-only service of 36 trains each way was withdrawn after 31st December 1932. On 29th July 1933 the branch ceased to be worked as a section, and became officially regarded as a siding worked by one engine in steam.

Kemp Town trains ran from the short easternmost bay at Brighton station, passed the locomotive works and traversed the Lewes line as far as Kemp Town Junction, just east of the 63 yds long Ditchling Road tunnel, a distance from Brighton of only 76 chains.

Top **View towards Kemp Town Tunnel from the station platform, 17th July 1931. The hollowing out of the chalk is clearly seen.** R.C. Riley Collection

Above **The Brighton Works shunter 377S in its Stroudley yellow livery on a Stephenson Locomotive Society special train, 23rd June 1956. Originally No.35** *Morden* **and BR No.32635, it was withdrawn in 1963.** R.C. Riley

From this point the branch was 1 mile 32 chains long. The curious layout at Lewes Road has been mentioned, although latterly for many years the line through the station was single and the station an unstaffed halt, tickets being issued by the train guard. Nevertheless the coal yard here survived until 14th June 1971. Immediately beyond Lewes Road the line became single and crossed the fine Lewes Road viaduct. Shortly after that there was a bridge over Hartington Road, on the south side of which the short-lived halt was sited. Thence the line went into a cutting, soon to enter Kemp Town tunnel, 1,024 yds in length. This assumed some importance in World War Two, when it was used nightly as an air raid shelter for multiple unit electric trains which were worked over the branch by a steam engine. This practice began in October 1941 and apart from a few weeks in May and June 1943 when London Road viaduct was closed as a result of bomb damage, it continued until May 1944.

Top **Class E4 0-6-2T No.32511 joins the branch at Kemp Town Junction, the 19-lever signal box probably dating back to the opening of the line. The fireman takes the train staff from the signalman, September 1953.** P. Hay

Above **The Small Radials of Class E3 were distributed throughout the former LBSC system until 1936 when they were concentrated on London depots mainly to shunt the yards at Bricklayers Arms, New Cross Gate and Norwood Junction. From 1949 they were gradually displaced by SR design 350hp diesels, 15211-36, hence the return to coastal and country sheds.** P. Hay

Another E4 Class 0-6-2T, No.32562, heads the freight consisting mainly of coal wagons, May 1957. Lewes Road viaduct is in the background and the brake van is on the bridge crossing Hartington Road, the site of the short-lived halt of that name. P. Hay

On emerging from the tunnel, Kemp Town station and goods yard were reached. The station consisted of one main platform with a run-round loop and a short bay effectively part of the goods yard. There was once a long canopy but this had disappeared after passenger closure as did the signal box. The station building was quite large, having much in common with other Sussex stations. Latterly it housed the Goods Agent and a coal order

office as well as being used as a dwelling. The extensive goods and coal yard never really achieved the aim of reducing traffic at the Brighton goods yard to any great extent. Originally two freight trains ran each weekday, but latterly this was reduced to one, normally hauled by a Class E4 0-6-2T. One of the last survivors of the class, No.32468, went out in style on 8th January 1963, when it went out of control on the falling grade into the station and embedded itself in the station house, which required to be shored up. Soon after the class became extinct and the freight train was worked by Class 08 or Class 09 diesel locomotives. The freight service continued, being finally closed on 14th June 1971.

Over the years a number of special passenger trains ran on the line, Sunday school excursions in pre-war days and railway enthusiasts specials after the war, the latter often worked by the once familiar Stroudley 'Terriers'. On 26th June 1971 a number of specials were run in aid of the Southern Railwaymen's Homes, these being worked by a three-coach DEMU. On removal of the track and demolition of the station, the site was sold to Brighton Council for industrial development including the rehousing of firms whose premises had been compulsorily acquired for road building or other schemes. The tunnel portal, locked up, can still be seen but the Lewes Road viaduct was demolished and little trace now remains of the branch.

Lewes Road station then in use by a builder's merchant, 23rd August 1952. Note the island platform at right. R.C. Riley

Planning the Pacifics
Derek Winkworth

The convoluted methods of designing, ordering and provision of the Southern Pacifics resulted from the SR's desire to get the best possible locomotives in the straitened circumstances of the second world war.

Above **The first of the Battle of Britain Class as originally proposed. Here it is seen in BR days as No.34051** *Winston Churchill.* BR (Southern Region)

The Southern Railway had an interesting habit of approving orders for locomotive construction to allow for a wide interpretation by the designer of the type and at the same time making such approval well in advance of the advent of the machine. For example, an order was placed on 7th October 1936 for two electric locomotives; the author recalls that, even in 1939, speculation was rife among the enthusiast fraternity as to how these engines would overcome 'gapping' on the third rail but it was not until mid-1941 that they first saw the light of day.

The way these matters were conducted may be seen from Minute B.2364 of the SR Board meeting of 18th December 1940, dealing with the 'Naming of New Express Locomotives'. This minute refers to the 20 Express Passenger Engines authorised by Rolling Stock Committee Minute 306 of 2nd March 1938 and approved by the Locomotive and Electrical Committee on 30th March 1938[1] and records that these were to be known as the 'Merchant Navy' class.

On New Year's Day 1940 the orders which stood uncompleted were:

Date of Order	Type
7th October 1936	2 electric
17th March 1937	20 0-6-0 goods tender
30th March 1938	20 4-6-2 exp passenger

To this list were then added, on 17th April 1940, 30 passenger tender engines, 20 goods tender engines and 25 4-6-2 mixed traffic engines for additional government traffic. These last 25 were placed on order at the behest of the Railway Executive Committee in expectation of increased and diverted cross-London freight traffic.

When the 1941 review was made on 23rd April of that year just one of these 117 locomotives had been produced. Notwithstanding, two further orders were then placed, the first for 20 steam locomotives of a type to be decided (this gave the Chief Mechanical Engineer, O.V. Bulleid, pretty wide latitude) and 15 diesel-electric locomotives.

By 1st January 1942 the list of uncompleted orders had seen some movement as shown below:

Date of Order	Type
7th October 1936	1 electric
17th March 1937	20 0-6-0 goods
30th March 1938	14 4-6-2 mixed traffic
17th April 1940	30 passenger tender
17th April 1940	20 0-6-0 goods
23rd April 1941	20 mixed traffic
23rd April 1941	15 diesel-electric shunting

25 4-6-2s on Government account altered to 20 2-8-0s

Forty-four of the Light Pacifics were named at official ceremonies. At Waterloo on 16th September 1947 three were so named, 21C154 *Lord Beaverbrook,* 21C165 *Hurricane* and 21C166 *Spitfire.* D.W. Winkworth

To swell the total, 50 mixed traffic locomotives were added under the 1942 construction programme plus one replacement for the engine (T14 class 4-6-0 No.458) bombed beyond economical repair at Nine Elms shed on 30th September 1940. There were orders, therefore, for not far short of 200 locomotives.

It was one thing for the Southern to carry on merrily ordering locomotives during the war but quite another to have the engines built. The Railway Executive Committee (REC) was the arbiter in the matter of locomotive construction and, although initially agreeing to the 1936, 1937 and 1938 orders being carried out as outstanding construction, prevailed upon the SR in September 1941 — following the furore surrounding the building of the 'Merchant Navy' class[2] — to postpone the second half of that order (rather than cancel it as first suggested) so that the uncompleted order would diminish in due course from 20 to 10. The REC agreed that for 1941/2 the SR should build 10 4-6-2s ('Merchant Navy' class); 40 0-6-0s (Q1 class) and 20 (later amended to 26) War Department 2-8-0 locomotives, all of which fell a long way short of the programme put forward by the company.

When the Southern came to consider construction for 1943 all that happened, so far as its own designs were concerned, was that the 1937 and 1940 orders for the Q1s and 10 of the 1938 'Merchant Navy' order had been completed leaving 127 SR locomotives to be built. This total was then advanced to 187 with 30 mixed traffic, 20 goods tender and 10 shunting tank engines recommended! There were then no fewer than 110 mixed traffic locomotives approved by the company.

Early in 1943 consideration was being given by the Ministry of War Transport (MoWT) and the REC as to whether the 1944 Locomotive

Building Programme should include mixed traffic engines as opposed to a heavy freight type. All companies preferred their own designs of a mixed traffic engine and Missenden, the SR General Manager, produced a memorandum for the REC putting forward the Southern's case in these terms:

SR 1944 Locomotive Building Programme:
Reasons for 30 Mixed Traffic Engines

1. The wartime augmentation of SR traffic (services' travel — British Railways — 26% of the duty, 22% of the leave and 28% of the travel paid for at time of booking originates on the SR. SR loaded wagon miles 30% in excess of pre-war) has to be carried not only over main trunk routes, but over secondary routes not available to the heaviest classes of engines. Such routes include the group of lines west of Exeter — 200 route miles, the Netley line (Portsmouth–Southampton), the Ringwood line (Southampton–Dorchester).

2. SR daily engine rosters include numerous instances of the same engine being used for both passenger and freight working during 24 hours. This mixed working is particularly in evidence west of Exeter. SR is still predominantly a passenger line — passenger traffic still accounts for 67% of total steam train miles of system.

3. Routes west of Exeter are heavily graded. Axle load has to be kept down to 18½ tons and 'hammer blow' eliminated in view of the construction of many bridges. Most modern type at present available dates from 1917 with a tractive effort of 25,000lb. Much of the traffic in the area has to be worked by relatively old 4-4-0 engines.

4. Growing and fluctuating war traffic can only be efficiently handled by a stock of relatively powerful mixed traffic engines. Further service requirements of major

importance are likely in West of England, and, apart from requirements on other sections, an engine of greater tractive effort than those now available with ample boiler capacity is essential in this area.

5. Mixed traffic engine proposed is same as 'Merchant Navy' class except in those parts in which it is essential for weight reductions to make a difference.
   (Examples of interchangeable parts then follow)

The tender will be a duplicate (in all details) of the existing Q1 tender. In fact — apart from the boiler — 85% of the locomotive will be the same as the 'Merchant Navy' class: even for the boiler the end plates of the inner and outer fireboxes will be identical with the 'Merchant Navy'. This interchangeability of parts will be of great value in connection with running shed repairs to proposed new engines and with the building and maintenance of 'Merchant Navy' engines. Moreover it is important that existing jigs and tools will be used in building lighter mixed traffic engines: this will speed up production.

6. The mixed traffic engines of other Companies are unsuitable for the SR system for one or more of the following reasons:–
   (a) Tractive effort too low compared with the proposed small 'Merchant Navy' engine (31,500lb.)
   (b) Route restrictions (for such reasons as width over cylinders, weight on driving wheels and hammer blow) would bar or greatly limit their use on those SR lines where a more powerful engine is now particularly required.

General Manager's Office
Waterloo
12.5.43

No.21C121, in its early un-named days when shedded at Ramsgate, passing Petts Wood Junction with a Charing Cross–Ramsgate via Dover train. D.W. Winkworth

'West Country' Class No.21C124, also in its early days at work on Ramsgate Depot's duty 470 which included a Charing Cross–Ramsgate service seen here at Sevenoaks (Tubs Hill). D.W. Winkworth collection

This special pleading on Missenden's part was duly forwarded to the MoWT by the REC on 18th May 1943 and was rewarded during August by agreement to the 1944 programme for the SR of 30 mixed traffic, 20 freight and 10 small shunting engines. So the germ of an idea mooted in January 1940[2] had at last come to fruition, although it was some time before the SR drawing office got down to putting the design on paper. The approved order of 17th April 1940 was allocated to the light 4-6-2s.

No further orders for locomotives were made by the SR in 1944 but in March 1945 a thorough review of the position was undertaken with the result that uncompleted orders were indicated as:

Date of Order	Type	To be completed by
7th October 1936	1 electric	May 1945
30th March 1938	8 4-6-2 mixed traffic ('Merchant Navy')	April 1945
17th April 1940	30 passenger (light 4-6-2)	25 by December 1946
23rd April 1961	20 4-6-2 mixed traffic (light 4-6-2)	October 1945
23rd April 1941	15 diesel-electric shunting	—
19th February 1942	50 mixed traffic (light 4-6-2)	December 1946
25th March 1943	30 mixed traffic	—
25th March 1943	20 goods tender	—
25th March 1943	10 shunting tank	December 1946
—	1 replacement for bombed engine	—

At that time unnamed but later named *Okehampton*, No.21C113 of Exmouth Junction heads a down express at Exeter Central in September 1946. R.C. Riley

From the above list it will be seen that there were orders available for 100 light 4-6-2s with another 30 approved in 1943 to cover more 'Merchant Navy' and light 4-6-2 examples, although in the event there appears to have been some juggling around with the sequence in completing the orders.

The first of the light 4-6-2 class, No.21C101 'Exeter', came out of works just too late in 1945 to assist in the war effort but was promptly allocated to Exmouth Junction shed for work on the lines west of Exeter as outlined in Missenden's submission of May 1943. Others of the class, known as 'West Country', followed to Exmouth Junction depot with the exception of Nos. 21C117 and 21C119 which were drafted, unnamed, to the Eastern Section shed of Stewarts Lane.

By one of those quirks of fate the wartime work for which the class had been envisaged in the West Country had suddenly evaporated and there was a greater need for power on the Eastern Section. At a meeting between the General Manager, Sir Eustace Missenden (as he had by then become), and the traffic officers on 13th February 1946 it was decided to progressively draft the new engines on to the Eastern Section with six at work by the end of February and a dozen by mid-May. The Traffic Manager considered it was inadvisable to introduce the engines more rapidly, partly on grounds of need for training in driving and maintenance and partly because of detrimental psychological reaction in the West of England if the locomotives were withdrawn from that area to work in Kent. Therefore, no transfers from Exmouth Junction shed were effected, 18 engines being kept in Devon with names appropriate for the area; new construction from No.21C121 onwards was allocated, without names attached, to the Eastern Section.

At a meeting on 18th December 1946 of the Locomotive, Carriage and Wagon and Electrical Committee Sir Eustace reported that it would be necessary for engines of the 'West Country' type to work for some years on the Eastern Section and it was considered that the next 40 engines, commencing with No.21C151, should bear names connected with the area. Various suggestions had been examined with the result that this batch of engines was to be known as the 'Battle of Britain' class. Names selected were Winston Churchill, Air Chief Marshal Lord Dowding, Air Chief Marshal Sir Keith Park, Lord Beaverbrook, Fighter Pilot, Hurricane, Spitfire, Tangmere, Kenley, Hawkinge, Croydon, Manston, Biggin Hill and Squadrons 25, 229, 257, 264, 222, 92, 605, 219, 422, 73, 615, 249, 41, 141, 66, 253, 145, 602, 17, 302, 46, 603, 74, 421, 501, 213 and 23. The Air Ministry had offered their co-operation.

The same committee was advised, at their meeting of 22nd October 1947, by the Air Ministry that Squadrons 421 and 422 did not take part in the Battle of Britain and that Squadron 302 was a Polish squadron without a badge registered. To replace these Fighter Command, Anti-Aircraft Command and Royal Observer Corps were included. The Secretaries of State for War and Air suggested that two engines should be named Sir Frederick Pile and Sir Archibald Sinclair; in agreeing to this the committee directed that these two engines should be taken from the previous 'West Country' batch (Nos.21C149 and 21C150) and then went on to approve names for Nos.21C131 to 21C148.

Right **No.21C110** *Sidmouth,* **one of the first batch of 'West Country' locos first allocated to Exmouth Junction shed, arriving at Salisbury on 29th June 1946 with the 10.25am Exeter Central–Waterloo train.** D.W. Winkworth

Centre Right **The 'West Country' which eventually headed the 'Battle of Britain' series. No.34049** *Anti-Aircraft Command* **arriving at Sidmouth Junction with the 9am Waterloo–Sidmouth/Exmouth on 23rd August 1958.** D.W. Winkworth

Bottom Right **Nameplate and badge of No.34049** *Anti-Aircraft Command.* D.W. Winkworth

This suggestion for two additional names upset an otherwise tidy number and name sequence. Instead of running to 21C150 as intended the 'West Country' list had to be truncated at 21C148. Furthermore, naming of the 'Battle of Britain' class had commenced with No.21C151 'Winston Churchill' on 11th September 1947 and eight other engines had already been christened at various ceremonies. Clearly to upstage 'Winston Churchill' as class leader by 'Sir Frederick Pile' and 'Sir Archibald Sinclair' was most undesirable so two 'oddities', in 'Anti-Aircraft Command' and 'Royal Observer Corps', preceded No.21C151. It was, therefore, by pure chance that the 'Battle of Britain' class started with No.21C149 and underlines the fact that there was no difference between 'West Country' and 'Battle of Britain' examples in their original form.

A few other observations may be made about the 'Battle of Britain' class names. It was decided not to include the Royal Air Force rank in the cases of Lord Dowding and Sir Keith Park. The name of Squadron 615, was originally allocated to locomotive No.34071 (in fact the nameplates were attached from April to August 1948) but was replaced by that of Squadron 601, the naming ceremony taking place on 16th September 1948. Originally the name of Squadron 601 had been assigned to No.34090 and when the change had been made this engine was re-allocated the name of Squadron 615, but on 8th October 1948 No.34082 was officially named '615 Squadron'. No.34082 had been selected to carry the name of Squadron 66 but this eventually appeared on the final member of the combined classes, No.34110, without accompanying badges, the sole example not so adorned. The name of Squadron 23 was not used at all.

In retrospect the 'Battle of Britain' naming sequence seems to have been done at random. The two oddities start the list, then four personalities, followed by 'Fighter Pilot', two RAF stations, two more personalities, four RAF Squadrons, one RAF Command, two aircraft types, four more RAF stations, then a run of 19 Squadrons, concluded by 'Sir Eustrace Missenden Southern Railway' and, after 18 'West Country' names, another personality and, finally, another Squadron. However, the naming of the 4-6-2s, large and small, is a subject in itself!

Sources:
Public Record Office, Kew: AN2 977, AN3 5, 7, 33, RAIL 645: 4, 29, 53, 54, 55, 56, 57, 58 92, RAIL 649: 55

Footnotes:
1. Philip Atkins, 'More Light on the Bulleid 4-6-2s', Railways South East, Vol.3 No.1 (in which doubt was cast on the date of 30th March 1938).
2. D.W. Winkworth, 'Attempts to Torpedo the Merchant Navy Class', Railways South East, Vol.2 No.3.

The author wishes to thank Philip Atkins for his useful comments.

An almost forgotten and never important branch line along the shore of the Colne estuary in Essex, the Wivenhoe and Brightlingsea was built for the carriage of sprats and oysters. Christopher Awdry traces its somewhat eventful history.

Wivna to Bricklesey
Christopher Awdry

It was not unusual that money for a railway project should have come from outside the area — a substantial amount of support for the Great Western Railway came from Liverpool, for instance, and much finance for Scottish railways came from England. But these were major undertakings, so perhaps it is strange that much of the backing for a short, localised, line such as the Wivehhoe & Brightlingsea should come from Yorkshire.

In 1860 George Bradley, with two financier friends, bought the Lordship of the Manor of Brightlingsea (Essex) — Bricklesey in local parlance. Bradley was a Castleford solicitor, who also owned a glassworks and made something of a speciality in buying manorial rights, along with his friend John Robinson, a banker from Pontefract. The third party in the deal was Edward Westwood, who came from Stourbridge and put up much of the money.

Brightlingsea — 'ea' being an old word for island, the name is thought to derive from 'Brihtric's island' — lies on the north shore of the Colne estuary, at the mouth of a wide creek. Its inhabitants, 2,585 of them in 1861, made their living from the sea, and had done for many years. Then, as now, a single road connected the community with the outside world, and St Osyth, nearby, was more important to it than Colchester or Wivenhoe. Between 1851 and 1861 the population of the St Osyth area fell by 133, but it is noticeable that in the years immediately after the railway was opened in 1866, Brightlingsea on its own increased its numbers by 500, and it continued to grow. The only later falls were to come in the decade of the Great War and in the 1930s.

The construction of railways was common enough during the 1860s, but at first glance a line along the north shore of the Colne estuary seems something of an oddity. Yet there was a very good and, as it turned out, a very lucrative reason. Sprats and oysters. The sprats which teemed in the estuary, were caught and landed at Brightlingsea, but this produce was used for nothing more than fish manure on the local fields. There must, it was thought, be a market for it inland if it could be got economically to Colchester. And if sprats could travel, why not oysters? Why, Colchester oysters might even become famous!

As in everything, of course, there was a snag. There was a rival concern, the Tendring Hundred Railway, which had already diverged from a branch to the Hythe, at Colchester, and was planning to extend to Wivenhoe, where it had bought a large tract of land between the station site and the river in order to provide "...a capacious wharf, with sidings... where the largest vessels trading to the port of Colchester would discharge their cargoes with facility."[1]

The Wivenhoe & Brightlingsea Railway obtained its Act on 11th July 1861[2], for a line from an end-on junction with the THR at Wivenhoe, then curving to the right and running for 5 miles 4 chains alongside the estuary to a terminus at Brightlingsea. Capital was fixed at £25,000, with additional borrowing powers for £8,000, but no borrowing was permitted until all the capital had been subscribed. Compulsory purchase powers for land expired after two years, but this at least presented no problem, since interested parties already owned more than half of the land that was required anyway.

The Brightlingsea promoters seem to have kept the whole thing fairly close to their chests, since in order to obtain their Act in 1861, the Application, Books of Reference and so on must have been submitted in November 1860. Yet what appears to have been the first public meeting about the undertaking took place only on 14th December 1860, at the Duke of Wellington Inn, Brightlingsea, when public support for the project was invited.[3] Mr Hugh C E Childers (MP for Pontefract) took the chair, and several interested parties explained why the railway was needed and how useful and

rewarding for shareholders it would be when it was built. The Assistant Engineer, James S. Cooke, apologised for the unavoidable absence of his superior, J. Olroyd Greaves, and said that the only expensive work in the line would be the bridge across Alresford Creek. He estimated a cost of £5,000 per mile, and suggested that the works should be carried out by the Company, thus saving contractor's costs. The Meeting noted the rival THR scheme as "...a valuable feeder..." and hoped that the scheme would be carried out "...to its full integrity." Alas, the relationship was not always to be so cordial.

Subscribers to the scheme are named in the Act as Hugh Culling Eardley Childers, Andrew Clarke, Richard Moxon (Ex-Mayor of Pontefract), Edward Williams (MD, Mayor of Colchester), James Edward Robinson, Edward Westwood, Hugh McDowall, James Grout, Robert Warwick, George Bradley, George Wyatt Digby, Robert Lufkin, Nathaniel Riches, George Edward Digby, John Coppin (Army Contractor) and Thomas Summersum. The first six named were elected first Directors, with Childers as Chairman. The new Company had pipped the Tendring Hundred Company at the post.

The last phase. The date is 2nd August 1959 and a Derby built DMU takes on a passenger or two for the journey inland. A.E. Bennett

But the THR put a brave face on things. It was, of course, protected by a number of provisions in its own Act,[4] which specified the site of the junction with the new line and gave authority to build and work any signalling in connection with the junction — expenses to be covered by the W&BR. There was also a clause specifying that if the THR laid double track, the first quarter-mile of the W&BR must be double also. The communication between the two lines was to be made at the expense of the Brightlingsea Company, under the supervision of the THR Engineer, who was Peter Bruff.

Progress on both projects was slow. The first sod of the Brightlingsea railway was cut on 21st September 1863 by Mrs Waters, the wife of the Rector of Wivenhoe, assisted by Sir Claude de Crespigny, who until lately had been on the Board of the THR and had transferred his allegiance. The ceremony was followed by a champagne lunch at the Park Hotel, Wivenhoe, when the Assistant Engineer predicted that the line could be finished in a year — the Contractor, William Munro, had been talking optimistically of six months. In point of fact it was to be a great deal longer than either expected.

On 29th February 1864 the Engineers reported that 2.5 miles of seawall had been built, and the line from Wivenhoe to Alresford Creek had been laid. Work on the bridge had begun, and 100 tons of iron lay on the ground there: the structure is referred to in documents severally as the iron bridge, swing bridge or Ford Bridge — it will usually be described here as the swing bridge. Shaws of Birmingham were responsible for it, and Paul Brown[5] suggests that this Midland connection may have come about through Edward Westwood, whose business interests were in that part of the country. The Great Eastern had agreed to contribute a third of the share capital, and £9,743 had so far been spent on the works[6]. By now however, the cost of the line was being put at £40,000, an ominous increase in only three years.

On 20th May Richard Moxon was elected as Chairman of the Company in the place of Childers. Moxon was the head of a successful Pontefract malting business, who had already been Mayor of that town twice, in 1858 and 1859, and was to hold the office twice more, in 1871 and 1876. A blunt and outspoken man, he nevertheless commanded great respect, particularly in his home town,

where he was to have a long record of public service almost until his death in December 1904.[7]

Moxon it was, then, who presided when an optimistic report was presented to the W&B shareholders in September 1864, and reported in *The Times* of 23rd of that month:-

"The earthworks of this line have reached an advanced stage and the ballasting will shortly be commenced. The heaviest portion of the undertaking is the iron bridge over Alresford Creek, the centre section of which is to open for the passage of barges and other craft using the channel. A good foundation has been obtained for this bridge at a less depth than had been anticipated and about one third of the side and roadway girders have been erected, so that the structure is expected to be complete early in 1865. The remainder of the line will then be ready for traffic."

What the report did not say — and in fairness, the Engineer may not have known — was that Munro was in financial difficulties. Soon it was obvious that his September 1864 deadline would not be met, and the THR, anxious to utilise the W&BR for a part of its own extension to Weeley, grew restive. If track was not laid by 1st November, the THR announced, it would build the line for itself and send the Brightlingsea Company the bill. At this juncture, the Tendring Hundred Company also recovered some of its capital by selling off, on 19th August 1864, the surplus land it would not now need for its quay at Wivenhoe.[8]

Munro's construction deadline was extended to January 1865 by the W&BR, but there was no way that he could meet the THR's November cut-off date. The THR went ahead as announced, and submitted its account — after ten years of wrangling over its accuracy, the W&BR eventually paid £7,000.

As a result of a fracas on the nearby Mistley, Thorpe & Walton Railway, Munro was declared bankrupt early in 1865. Several ultimata for completion went unmet, and the Board resolved on 7th June[9] to take over the works and to defend the case which Munro was preparing to bring against the Company. A suggestion has been made that Peter Bruff was enlisted to complete the work, but a report from Robert Sinclair (Engineer of the GER) had been read to a Directors' meeting on 27th February that year[10]. Bruff is not mentioned in the Company Minutes at any point, and it seems more likely, to this writer at least, that it was Sinclair who took over.

Munro's replacement was Frederick Furniss, whose tender was accepted on 1st July,[11] and at the same time a tender of £767 was accepted from William Pickford Wilkins for completion of the swing bridge. This Wilkins did during the year, and on 14th December payments to him of £150 and £403 3s 3d were passed by the Board. Furniss was not so fortunate though, for in October there was an extensive slip "...near a viaduct over Alresford Creek."[12] There was an inevitable delay while this was made good, and the market price of the Brightlingsea shares fell. With perfect timing the Great Eastern Railway stepped in and bought a third of them.

Col. Yolland inspected the line for the Board of Trade in late November or early December, "...paying particular attention to the large swing bridge ... but no date has yet been fixed for the opening of the line."[13] After curving to the right away from Wivenhoe, the line ran straight for about a mile until it reached the estuary shore. Another mile close to the waterline, with woods on the landward side, led to a climb on to the swing bridge, and beyond this the embankment fell away again. There was a timber bridge in this section, later replaced by embankment, and then the railway curved left to head due south-east and straight. This length was exposed on both sides, and must have been horribly uncomfortable for the engine crews in any sort of bad weather. Bateman Tower stood ahead, but before reaching it the line crossed the Wooden Bridge, a short length of timber trestle causeway — still visible, incidentally. Just beyond it the railway swung sharp left through ninety degrees towards the town which was its destination, and which had in fact already been visible for some time on the left-hand side.

Brightlingsea station was built on marshland at the southern end of the town, as close as possible to the quays, which, it was hoped, would bring the line a lucrative livelihood. It was of spartan construction, with a twin-gabled overall canopy of timber and roofing-felt, supported in the centre by a row of metal columns. The single platform, set to the south-east of the line, was three feet high, there was a water-tank for the engines and a garden for the stationmaster. A siding and goods dock lay to the north-west of the station.

Three days before the line opened, at a meeting at the Cups Hotel, Colchester, the Directors of the Wivenhoe & Brightlingsea Railway sealed an Agreement that the GER should work their line.[14] Terms were at a rate of 40%, and the Agreement, ratified by Parliament on 16th July 1866,[15] also covered working and maintenance of the line by the GER and agreed powers for lease, transfer or sale to that Company. Extra capital of £15,000 was also authorised, with additional borrowing powers for £5,000, though not until the additional capital was accounted for.

On Tuesday 17th April 1866, at 11am, a special train left London carrying Directors of both the W&BR and the GER to the new station at Brightlingsea. Sir Claude de Crespigny, as had been arranged, met them at Wivenhoe, and accompanied them towards the line's terminus. A halt was made en route to inspect the swing bridge. This was 430 feet long, with a centre span that swung through 90 degrees, resting on timber piles at its outer ends. There was a speed limit of 10 miles per hour for traffic crossing it, a restriction later amended to 5mph. The structure came to be heartily disliked by the locals, who claimed that it swayed in a high wind. The speed limit didn't help either, because the fact that it was necessary proved, to them anyway, that the bridge was unsafe.

The party was met at Brightlingsea by the stationmaster, Mr William Abbot, and other local personages, and an oyster luncheon was consumed in the goods area of the station. Fortunately it was a fine day — the station had few bad-weather facilities. The guests were back in Colchester by 5pm, where they enjoyed "...a sumptuous dinner..." at the Cups Hotel.[16] A slightly jarring note was hit during the speeches when a GER Director alluded somewhat tactlessly to the amount of capital supplied by his Company. The line was opened for public use on the next day.

It wasn't long before the GER was making its presence felt. In May it requested that, "...an Engine and Tender Shed capable of holding an Engine and Tender, a small Lockup for Stores, a suitable pit, waterpipes and coke stage..." be provided at Brightlingsea, and suggested the provision of telegraph also. All were acceded to by the W&B Board,[17] though the building of the engine shed was postponed in December and offered for tender in March the next year. This may well have been because the Company was harder up than usual, for there had been another heavy slip of the embanking near the swing bridge in July.

"The recent heavy rains," reported *The Times* of 4th July 1866, "having caused a portion of this line to give way near Ford's Bridge it had been found necessary to suspend the traffic, and, unfortunately, an omnibus, which was employed to continue the communication by road, was upset, and several passengers were more or less injured. One gentleman, Mr Surridge, an interpreter from the Vice-Consul's Office in Harwich, was severely cut about the head, while another sustained a fracture of the collar-bone."

Furniss must have put this problem right fairly swiftly, for two months later share-holders were told that traffic receipts for both freight and passengers were good and improving. The report hoped that at the end of the current half-year it might be possible "...to make a satisfactory dividend."[18] Alas, the first dividend was not to be declared for five years.

It was not only the works which caused the Company trouble. Cooke, the Assistant Engineer, presented an account to the Board for £26 5s 9d, which was passed "...to be paid, but get as much deducted as possible."[19] The Minutes are silent as to the nature of the difficulty, but Cooke appears to have brought some sort of case against the Company, for there is a note nine months later that the action is to be defended by the London firm of Swann & Co.

There was also to be a long-running dispute between the Company and the GER over mileage claims against the Tendring Hundred Company for traffic over the quarter mile of line between Wivenhoe station and Brightlingsea Junction. This dragged on until 1875.

In 1874 the W&B became dissatisfied with the way the GER was working the line, and one of the Directors, George Bradley was requested to write[20] to that Company, giving notice that it was, "...trespassing over our line..." On 21st February Bradley and the Company Secretary were told to prepare to work the line with horses until other arrangements could be made, and to "...procure carriages, wagons and employ such men and do all necessary acts for the working of the line." This was, it seems, not a success, for the next thing was that Bradley was offered the line on condition that he guarantee the payment of the debenture loans and interest due at the time. If he should decline to do this, he was empowered, with the Company Chairman, to negotiate with the GER for the disposal of its interest in the Brightlingsea Company.[21]

In January 1875 the Great Eastern was asked to lower its working expenses, on the grounds that the price of coal, iron and other materials had gone down. The GE countered in August by asking the W&B to reduce its passenger fares. This the W&B declined to do. Thirteen months later the Great Eastern offered terms — presumably revised — but a Directors' Meeting Minute[22] reads:-

"...Mr Bradley was requested to ascertain the best terms he can for working the line, and unless more satisfactory terms than at present can be obtained, the Company work the line themselves."

At the next meeting Bradley reported that not only would the GE insist on 70% for expenses, but that it "...proposed to take the line on payment only of the interest on the debentures..." He had therefore, he told his fellow-Directors, bought an engine from Hudswell Clarke & Rogers of Leeds for £1,290 and "...two composite carriages, one with break (sic), of Messrs Craven Brothers ...at the sum of £790, and also a small wooden station."

This last also came from Craven's at a cost of £54 10s and was for the provision of independent accommodation at Wivenhoe, where a Mr Pattison was appointed station-master. On 22nd July 1876 the Board made the final arrangements for working its line from 1st August, and necessary work at Wivenhoe was directed to be done "...for the loading of passengers and Goods there and the interchange of Traffic."

The major engineering feature. The swing bridge from the south over Alresford Creek. The timber piling on which the swing span rested when open can be seen on the left. Paul Brown collection

Within a year it was clear that this self-help was not a success, and a Directors' meeting on 27th July 1877 resolved that the GER should resume working the line as early as possible on the following terms:-

"1. That the Great Eastern Railway Company work the line to 1st June next at 70% upon the Gross receipts.

"2. That from 1st June next at 60%.

"3. The engine and two carriages to be taken over by the Great Eastern Railway Company, also the Stores taken by this company, from their company, and other stores this Company has since purchased."

Peace seemed to have been restored at last. During the summer of 1881 the GE requested that, in view of the increase in excursion traffic, the platform at Brightlingsea should be lengthened and "...other alterations made."[23] These are unspecified in the Minute Book, but the W&B Directors resolved that the work should be done — the GE actually did it, and were paid £244 19s 1d.

Perhaps it was the excursionists that made the difference, for from August the next year the W&B paid its first dividend on Preference Shares of 1.75% or £1 15s (£1.75) per share.

On 27th February 1886 comes the first mention of a man who served the railway for 50 years — George Ruffell. He had joined the Company 12 years before, and was by now an overseer; his account for £50 for work in "...protecting the banks..." and supervising the GE work at Brightlingsea was accepted and paid without demur. He was appointed stationmaster at Brightlingsea in 1900, a post he retained until his retirement.

Two years later the Great Eastern pointed out anomalies in passenger fares, and the Board agreed to a reduction. It was also stated that in order to compete with other ports the rate for the carriage of oysters had been reduced from 20s (£1) to 15s (75p) per ton — perhaps this is why the next dividend fell to 1⁵⁄₁₂% from the 2⅜ of the previous six months.

It was on 22nd September 1888 that the W&BR Board made what may be seen as perhaps its most momentous decision — to sell out to the Great Eastern. As it turned out this was much more easily resolved than done. Moxon and Bradley met the GER on 4th December and discussed terms which Moxon recommended his own company's shareholders to accept. The GER decision was left until representatives had had a chance to inspect the line. Clearly they did not much like what they saw, for the GE declined the W&B terms and offered £28,000, claiming that this was a 25-year projection of earnings based on the average income that it had made from the line over the last three years.

A further meeting at first failed to increase the GE's offer. The fact that the W&B shares had recently gained in value was pointed out however, and by the end of the meeting Mr Birt, for the GER, "...intimated that the offer might be increased but not by very much."[24] The W&B itself maintained that its value was the GE's 1889 net earnings of £1,243 6s 8d (£1243.33), which, when multiplied by 25, came out at £31,075, not including the freehold. By 31st January 1891 the Brightlingsea Company had fixed its asking price at £40,000, subject to Parliamentary arrangement and agreement by the GE before 21st February next. The GE remained adamant, and the W&B Secretary wrote again, pointing out that traffic had increased since the offer of £28,000 had been rejected.

Above **The W&B's only loco, 0-6-0ST** *Resolute* **built by Hudswell Clark in 1876, taken over by the GER and withdrawn 1888.** Paul Brown collection

Below **The upper composite coach came from the Thetford & Wotton Railway and was destroyed in the fire of 30th December 1901. The lower was bought from Cravens when the W&B planned independence. It was taken over by the GER and renumbered 126.** Paul Brown collection

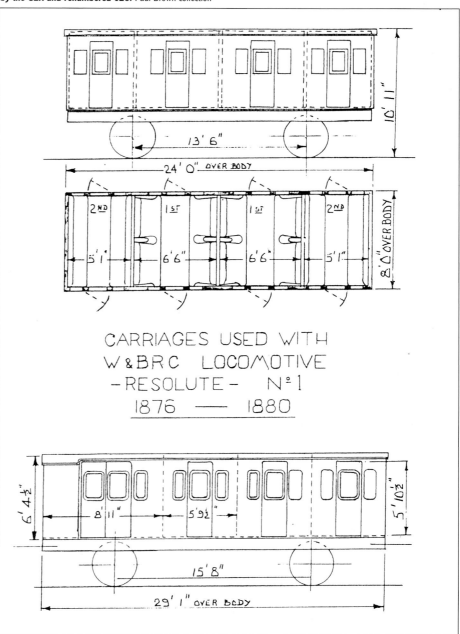

CARRIAGES USED WITH W&BRC LOCOMOTIVE -RESOLUTE- Nº 1 1876 —— 1880

Period		Dividend Declared	Paid per share
Six months to	5/8/1882	1¾%	£1.15s (£1.75)
	3/2/1883	1½%	£1.10s (£1.50)
	4/8/1883	1¾%	£1.15s (£1.75)
	6/2/1884	2%	£2
	9/8/1884	1½%	£1.10s (£1.50)
	7/2/1885	2⅛%	£2.2s.6d (£2.12)
	8/8/1885	1¾%	£1.15s (£1.75)
	6/2/1886	1⅔%	£1.13s.4d (£1.67)
	27/8/1886	1⅔%	£1.13s.4d (£1.67)
	5/2/1887	2½%	£2.10s (£2.50)
	6/8/1887	1⅔%	£1.13s.4d (£1.67)
	4/2/1888	2⅜%	£2.7s.6d (£2.37)
	4/8/1888	1⁵⁄₁₂%	£1.8s.4d. (£1.42)
	2/2/1889	2⁵⁄₁₂%	£2.8s.4d. (£2.42)
	8/8/1889	1⁹⁄₁₀%	£1.18s (£1.90)
	1/2/1890	3%	£3
	2/8/1890	2⅓%	£2.6s.8d (£2.33)
	31/1/1891	3⅕%	£3.4s (£3.20)
	1/8/1891	2⅓%	£2.6s.8d (£2.33)
	30/1/1892	3½%	£3.10s (£3.50)
	30/7/1892	3%	£3
	1/1893	2%	£2
	7/1893	2½%	£2.10s (£2.50)

Left **Wivenhoe & Brightlingsea Railway — Dividends declared on Preference Shares, 1882 to 1893.**

Below **A GER 2-4-0 locomotive (later LNER Class E4) prepares to leave Brightlingsea on 3rd September 1906, the day the new station opened.**
Paul Brown collection

But the W&BR had to climb down. A sum of £31,000 was suggested, and the GE, on 19th March, offered "…between £30,000 and £32,000, but on no consideration would they be prepared to pay more." The Board agreed to accept this offer on 3rd June, and the shareholders ratified the decision at an Extraordinary Meeting, held in the Chairman's office at Pontefract on 27th February 1892. The conveyance transferring the line to the Great Eastern was completed on 17th January 1894. The W&B's engine disappeared into the GER system as No.208, but the carriages were retained on the branch until withdrawal in 1898. All things considered, the GE probably got a bargain, though in later years British Railways was to claim large losses and overheads as an excuse for closure.

It remained only to repay the shareholders. The last General Meeting was held in Pontefract on 20th October 1894, and the final Directors' meeting took place, also in Pontefract, on 30th March 1895 — after all payments to shareholders there was £16 12s 2d (£16.61) left in the kitty, and this was divided between the three remaining Directors, Moxon, Robinson and Westwood. The seal of the Company was despatched to the Great Eastern, and it was recorded in the Minute Book that "…the Company is now wholly dissolved and ceases to exist." Richard Moxon who had been a Director of the Company throughout its life, was given a cordial vote of thanks for 31 years of service, and it seems somehow appropriate that the final words in the book should be his signature.

So now the line belonged to the Great Eastern Railway, but there were few immediate changes. In 1900 Richard Sargent, the stationmaster at Brightlingsea resigned. He had entered railway service in 1858 and served as stationmaster at Bury St Edmunds, Kennett, Buntingford and Elmswell, before coming to Brightlingsea in March 1883. He now took over the cartage agency in the town on behalf of the GE, a post he still held at the time of his death, on 11th May 1912.[25]

The most sensational event in the line's history took place on Monday 30th December 1901. William Beaumont, engine cleaner, nearing the station at Brightlingsea at 11pm to begin duty, was startled to see a red glow surrounding it. Rushing to the platform he found a carriage well alight. Realising he could do little single-handed, he ran to an engine and roused the town by sounding its whistle. Ruffell, recently appointed stationmaster in succession to Sargent, arrived first, and Beaumont, showing considerable bravery, uncoupled the burning carriage from that which stood between it and the engine. He then drove the untouched carriage and engine clear of the blaze. The timber station building offered no resistance, and was soon past saving. Within two hours all had gone, save "…some twisted ironwork and the remains of some automatic vending machines."[26]

The Times report of 1st January 1902 allots Beaumont's bravery to Ruffell, and mentions the rescue of "…much valuable rolling stock", though this seems unlikely, given the lack of facilities at Brightlingsea. It also propounds a theory that the fire started in a porter's room, but fails to suggest how it could have been transferred to a carriage. There was a strong local belief, however, that since the facilities at the station were gener-

ally agreed to be abysmal, someone served everyone else a good turn by setting a match to it. It seems likely that we shall never know for certain, but we do know that the carriage which perished in the blaze was No.125, inherited from the Thetford & Watton Railway in 1879. It was a four compartment composite, 24 feet long.

The contractors for the new station were W Pattinson & Co, of Rushington, whose tender was £12,053, but who actually completed the work for considerably less. After a period when Brightlingsea passengers had to use a temporary structure on a new site to the south-east of the old one (which became a goods depot), this was replaced with a new building. The station still had only a single platform, but it was a definite improvement on its predecessor, having not only a waiting room, but a refreshment room too. It opened without ceremony on 3rd September 1906, and the line settled down to a period of quiet.

The Great Eastern was not backward in attempting to attract business to its branch lines. "For the benefit of those who delight in yachting," ran a report in *The Railway Magazine* of September 1905, no doubt culled

from a GE Press Release, "every Friday and Saturday cheap first and third class return tickets are issued from Liverpool Street to Brightlingsea by all trains, available for return by any of the advertised trains on any day up to and including the Tuesday following the date of issue. The tickets are available also to and from Wyvenhoe (a spelling of the name in use by the GER between 1879 and 1911). The third class fare for the double journey is only three half-crowns (7s 6d, or 37p) and disciples of Lipton (so far as yachting is concerned) doubtless find in the cheap rail journey an additional excuse for getting away from town to the pleasant rendezvous of their favourite pastime on the Essex coast."

For those who, like this author, are at first puzzled by the Lipton allusion, it refers to the Sir Thomas of that ilk, who not only established a chain of grocery stores, but also, in his youth, competed as a yachtsman in the America's Cup.

Commonwealth troops from Australia, New Zealand and Canada were billeted at Brightlingsea during the Great War, and doubtless contributed substantially to the revenue of the line. There were also, it must be said, a number of servicemen who simply climbed on the evening train at Brightlingsea, having 'forgotten' to buy a ticket. A custom of lengthy ticket checks was established at Wivenhoe to counter such memory lapses. A guard was put on the swing bridge, in case the enemy decided to blow it up, but it remained unmolested.

There was some wartime excitement though, other than that provided by the visiting troops, when the Wooden Bridge just outside Brightlingsea caught fire on an afternoon in 1915: stationmaster Ruffell mobilised a team which soon put it out. It probably started as a result of an engine cinder, but many locals preferred to believe that it was something more warlike. The refreshment room closed, ostensibly for the duration, primarily because of the food shortage, but also because it was said to be required for use as an emergency hospital for war-wounded. It was used as a hospital only by local people, but never re-opened as a refreshment room, becoming part of the stationmaster's house when hostilities ceased.

In 1922 Brightlingsea signalbox was removed, and from then on points were controlled by lineside levers. Almost two years after the Grouping, on 31st October 1924, George Ruffell retired. He had been stationmaster at Brightlingsea for 24 years and had been a railwayman for 50 — at a ceremony in Brightlingsea he was presented with an aneroid barometer and an illuminated address.

During the 1930s there was an incident on the swing bridge when track-walker Arthur Nice noticed one morning that the rails on the moving span were three inches out of alignment. Apparently a sand barge had hit the bridge in fog during the night. Nice ran to the Pilotman's cottage, only to find that the early-morning train had already left Brightlingsea. So he ran back across the bridge in time to wave the engine driver to a halt and avert what could have been a very unpleasant accident.

The original passenger service along the line was four trains each way daily, one of which was mixed, but this increased as Brightlingsea expanded. By 1890 eight trains were running each way, and two or three extras were being added on Sundays for the

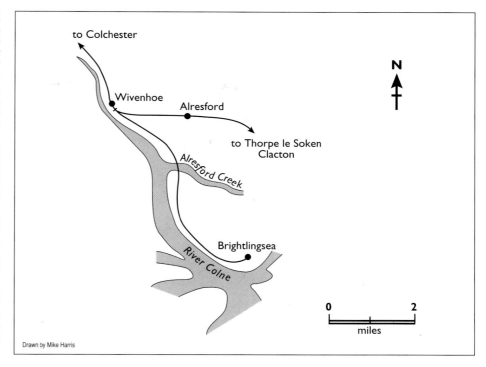

Drawn by Mike Harris

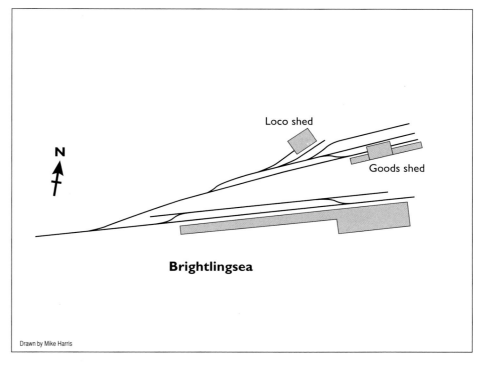

Brightlingsea

Drawn by Mike Harris

benefit of the excursionists. Cuts were made to the service for reasons of economy early in the First World War, and by the time peace came the GE timetable was showing four trains a day in each direction, a similar pattern to that which had started the branch off in 1866. By the mid-1930s however the service was back to 11 trains each way on weekdays, and the 1937 winter timetable shows no less than 13, with four on Sundays. This was probably the zenith, though even in 1947 seven trains ran each way on Sundays.

Many different locomotives worked these trains, but perhaps the longest-lasting of them were the Class E4 2-4-0s around the turn of the century, the 2-4-2 tank engines of Class F3 between the Wars, and from 1939 to 1957 the Class J15 0-6-0s. Diesel multiple units were introduced on 4th March 1957, and served until the end.

Flooding has been a major hazard along this coast for many years, and since it ran on embankment along the estuary shore, the Wivenhoe to Brightlingsea line had its share of troubles. There were floods in 1874, 1876 and 1882, but the first serious breach in the railway occurred in 1897, when the 2.47pm arrival at Brightlingsea was stranded 200 yards from the station. The passengers were ferried to the town by rowing boat, and it was several days before the line could be repaired. In 1901 the service was suspended for several days, and again in 1903. On 30th December 1904 a mile of track between Wivenhoe and the swing bridge was washed away. The GE at this time seriously considered abandoning the branch, but pressure from the Brightlingsea end won the day. The service was interrupted for three weeks. There was widespread flooding along the east coast in

In BR days, on 7th July 1956, J15 0-6-0 No.65432 takes on water before working the 4.48pm train to Colchester St Botolphs. R.M. Casserley

Looking in the other direction. The Colne estuary lies beyond the water column. The coal yard was still active. E.H. Sawford

August 1912, but this time Brightlingsea escaped.[27] In April 1949 the service was suspended for a while, but it was the great flood of 1953 which almost supplied the *coup de grace*. On 1st February Brightlingsea returned to being an island, and the arguments for and against retaining the line raged throughout the summer. On this occasion the 'fors' won, and amidst great local jubilation the line re-opened on 7th December, after extensive repairs had been carried out.

It was not, in the end, floods that caused the line's demise. Traffic fell away during the 1950s, and the Beeching Report recommended closure, largely, one suspects, on account of the expense of keeping the swing bridge in repair. Once again the battle — not for nothing did Paul Brown call his first book about the line *The Fighting Branch* — was taken up by the locals, and though the conflict was again an extended one there was no reprieve this time. At 7.30pm on 14th June 1964 a two-car diesel unit driven by Harold Bloes, who had worked on the line for 45 years, left Brightlingsea and headed towards 'Wivna' for the last time. It rounded the curve by the Bateman Tower, dwindled into the distance between marsh and estuary and finally disappeared behind the trees.

While there was still track the locals had hope, but lifting began on 11th November, and in 1967 the swing bridge was demolished — or most of it anyway. Today the tubular end-piers, a pair on either side of Alresford Creek, provide the most tangible reminder of a line once full of character and now fading in memory.

For their help in the preparation of this article, the author gratefully thanks staff at Brightlingsea and Colchester Museums, public libraries in Colchester and Pontefract, all who have supplied pictures, David Taylor of the Great Eastern Railway Society, and Paul Brown, whose book about the branch has been a source of much information, and is, it is hoped, to be republished shortly.

1. *Essex Standard*, 3 Oct. 1862, reporting the Shareholders meeting held on 27 Sept. 1862.
2. 24/25 Victoria, c.119 (11th Jul. 1861).
3. *Essex Standard*, 21st Dec. 1860.
4. 22/23 Victoria, c.119. (13th Aug 1859).
5. Paul Brown, *Wivenhoe & Brightlingsea Railway*, (Ian Henry Publications, Edn 1986).
6. *The Times*, 7th Mar 1864.
7. *Pontefract & Castleford Express*, 17th Dec 1904.
8. Essex Record Office (Colchester) 254.
9. W&BR Minutes, PRO RAIL758.1
10. Idem.
11. Idem.
12. *The Times*, 30th Oct 1865.
13. *The Times*, 5th Dec 1865.
14. W&BR Minutes, 14th Apr 1866
15. 29/30 Victoria, c.213.
16. *Essex Standard*, 21st Apr 1866.
17. W&BR Minutes, 26th May 1866.
18. *The Times*, 3rd Sep 1866.
19. W&BR Minutes, 5 Sep 1867.
20. Idem, 31st Jan 1874.
21. Idem, 28th Mar 1874.
22. Idem, 26th Feb 1876.
23. Idem, 6th Aug 1881.
24. Idem, 1st Feb 1890.
25. GER Magazine Vol 2.
26. Paul Brown op. cit.
27. GER Magazine Vol 2.

The somewhat dilapidated engine shed at Brightlingsea in April 1949. Real Photographs

The estuarine scene. The 4.48pm to Colchester nears the southern end of the swing bridge on 7th July 1956. R.M. Casserley

Right **Wivenhoe looking towards Brightlingsea on 7th July 1956.** R.M. Casserley

Steam in the Smoke
Fred Ivey

Emerging in a cloud of steam from the City Widened Lines tunnel at Kings Cross, N2 69549 enters the old wooden platform alongside the East Coast Main Line Terminus. The 0.6.2T is hauling an evening rush hour train from Moorgate to Hertford North. These former GNR/LNER locomotives were the mainstay of the Kings Cross and City local services. The young lady looks at her watch hoping to find that her train home has arrived on time.

2.6.2T 40024 arrives at Aldersgate and Barbican City Widened Lines, with an evening business train which has started from Moorgate, bound for northern suburbs on the former Midland Railway line. The locomotive is fitted with condensing apparatus allowing it to operate over the largely tunnel CWL, today part of Thameslink. There is little shelter from the elements, the overall roof having been removed a few years before. As a result of modern development in the area, the station is today merely called Barbican.

'Schools' Class 4.4.0 30918 *Hurstpierpoint* pulls away from Clapham Junction with a Central Section special train, possibly a Sunday Ramblers Excursion.

During the last days of the Alexandra Palace branch, an N2 0-6-2T running bunker first, picks up speed and leaves the tunnel south of Highgate Station with a train to Finsbury Park. Shortly afterwards on 3rd July 1954 the last passenger train ran, the line lingering on for the transfer of Underground cars to and from the Northern City Line at Highgate Depot. This was in stark contrast to the unrealised plan to extend the Northern Line by this route to Muswell Hill and Alexandra Palace. From the point where the photograph was taken, to Finsbury Park, there is today a public footpath.

Under the watchful eye of the signalman, a wartime built Austerity Class Q1 0.6.0 passes Bollo Lane Crossing signal box, just beyond South Acton, with a train of insulated meat containers. Whilst extremely ugly in appearance, the Q1s were versatile and efficient machines. Although usually seen on freight working, they were occasionally used on passenger trains. The first of the class restored as Southern Railway C1 is in use on the Bluebell Railway.

Drummond LSWR 0-4-4T Class M7 on an empty stock working to Walton-on-Thames passes Queens Road Battersea in the late 1950s, 4-EPB stock alongside. The station retained its name long after Queens Road itself became Queenstown Road, but was finally renamed in 1980.

Just a stone's throw from the former Great Western locomotive depot, Old Oak Junction signal box was on the North London line between Willesden High Level and Acton Wells Junction. The exchange sidings to the left were served by London Midland and Southern locomotives, being a northern outpost for the latter. G16 4.8.0T 30495, one of a class of former LSWR/SR locomotives, starts its train of small wagons probably bound for the Feltham marshalling yard, at which locomotive depot the G16's were based. The signal base has long since gone and where the sidings were there are now runnng lines connecting Willesden to Acton and to the former Southern system at Kew.

Rebuilt Merchant Navy locomotive 35028 *Clan Line* accelerates through Vauxhall with the Down Bournemouth Belle Pullman train. After withdrawal from BR service *Clan Line* was saved for preservation and in the eighties was a frequent performer on main line special trains. Former Southern Railway lamp posts and station name signs recall earlier days.

The Southampton & Netley Railway – A Branch Line Transformed

Edwin Course

Railways to hospitals are by no means uncommon, but with one important exception they have consisted of independent branch lines, and have not formed part of the railway system. The important exception is the Southampton and Netley Railway, opened between Southampton and the great military hospital at Netley in 1866.

At the time the Southampton and Netley Railway was conceived, two lines had been opened serving Southampton. In 1840, the main line between London and Southampton was completed. This was a classic line of the first generation of railways, its main purpose being to serve the port rather than the town. The Southampton and Dorchester Railway followed in 1847. Despite its title, there were hopes that the line would form part of a route to the West of England. In the event, this role was achieved by the line via Salisbury, but at least part of the Southampton and Dorchester developed as a route to the new town of Bournemouth. Predictably, the London and Southampton had terminated at a site adjoining the docks, so it was not practical for the extension to Dorchester to achieve an end-on junction. Instead, it branched off short of the terminus, and until 1857, when a spur line was opened, all trains going beyond Southampton had to reverse in the terminal station.

In the same way, the Southampton and Netley branched off at St Denys, about one and a half miles in the London direction from the terminus. Although it was opened in 1866, it was 1889 when the anticipated extension to Fareham was completed, giving access to Portsmouth, and for its first 23 years the Netley line was no more than a branch line. Bearing in mind the circuitous route between Southampton and Portsmouth via Eastleigh, it is perhaps not surprising that the first

plans were for a more direct link between the two towns, rather than a branch to a hospital. In 1859, the Southampton and Fareham Railway proposed such a line. There were two rivers to cross. A bridge was to be constructed over the River Hamble, but the line did not cross the Itchen. Instead it terminated on the left bank at Woolston, opposite the town of Southampton, and traffic would have completed its journey by way of the floating bridge of 1836. Needless to say, this scheme was supported by the proprietors of the Itchen Bridge Company, but it failed to gain sufficient backing and was withdrawn. Other schemes followed, all of which included provision for serving the hospital under construction at Netley.

The Royal Naval Hospital at Haslar in Gosport had been opened in 1754, but it was not until 1856, after the end of the Crimean War, that Queen Victoria laid the foundation stone 'of a Military Hospital for the reception of sick and wounded soldiers of her army.' It was to be a vast, monolithic structure with a frontage of 1424 feet, which reflected architectural status, rather than medical considerations — in fact, Miss Nightingale did not approve.

However, the Royal Victoria Hospital was completed in 1863. It could be reached by water, and it was anticipated that most of the sick and wounded would reach the hospital by boat. On discharge, they would require land transport.

Above **An ambulance train at the hospital platform, with buildings of the Royal Victoria Hospital in the background. The locomotive is M7 Class No.106, built at Nine Elms Works in 1905 and demolished in 1960. The photograph was probably taken during the First World War.** Lens of Sutton

The initial aim of the Southampton and Netley Railway, authorised in 1861, was to link Southampton to the new hospital. Its Act of Parliament specified 'a Railway between the London and South Western Railway at or near to that Railway at St Denis (sic) near Southampton and the Military Hospital at Netley.' The company appears to have been independent as neither its engineer, J.M. Harkness, nor its London solicitor, G.T. Porter, were directly connected with the LSWR or the LBSCR. Among the backers was Thomas Chamberlayne, who owned a good deal of the land on the east side of the Itchen, through which the line was to run. Beyond the river crossing, a fairly direct line to Netley was planned, climbing at 1 in 75 to pass through the village of Bitterne. Emboldened by their initial success, the S & N then deposited plans for an extension to Fareham which, associated with a spur to St Denys, facing Southampton, would have formed part of a through route between Southampton and Portsmouth. At this stage, the London and South Western moved in, and Harkness was replaced by LSW engineers, Tolmé and Galbraith. Formal absorption of the S & N by the LSW was authorised by an Act of 1864, but in practice the LSW took over in 1862. A new survey was carried out by Tolmé. Instead of the steep climb and deep cutting through Bitterne Village, beyond the bridge over the Itchen the line followed the left bank to a point in Woolston near the floating bridge terminal. This did not of course avoid a climb up from the river, but it did reduce the gradient to 1 in 97 and also involved less cutting. (The plans show a gradient of 1 in 100). Instead of the extension to Fareham, beyond Netley the proposed line ran down to a quay on the River Hamble. The revised alignment was authorised in 1863, the acquisition of land was proceeded with and the contract for construction was let to Messrs Sharpe and Sons of Westminster. The final adjustment was proposed in 1863 and authorised in 1864. The junction had faced London, but in its final form it faced Southampton with consequential adjustments to the position of the bridge and the alignment down to the river bank. Apart from the extension to Hamble Quay, the line was opened on 5th March 1866.

Below Sholing Station before the doubling of the line in 1910. The top of the SM's house appears above the bridge. Doubling necessitated the full use of the bridge hole and the demolition of the existing station.

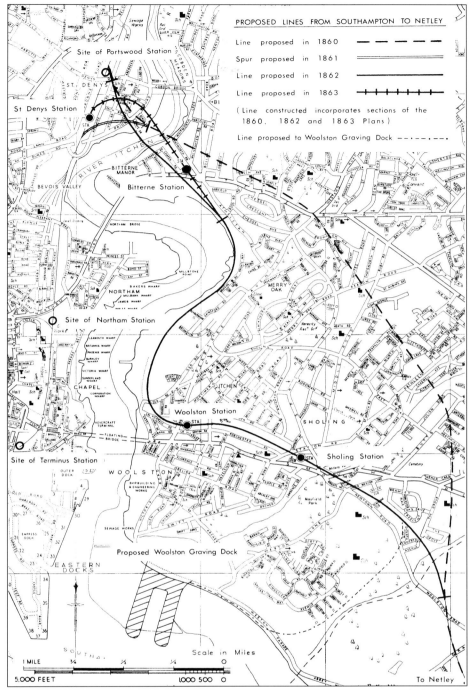

PROPOSED LINES FROM SOUTHAMPTON TO NETLEY

Line proposed in 1860	—— —— ——
Spur proposed in 1861	=========
Line proposed in 1862	—————————
Line proposed in 1863	+—+—+—+—+

(Line constructed incorporates sections of the 1860, 1862 and 1863 Plans)

Line proposed to Woolston Graving Dock —·—·—·—·—

Woolston Station viewed from the forecourt in January 1973. The building of 1866, with accommodation for passengers below and for the stationmaster above, is now Listed Grade II. Apart from the cutting away of part of the valance of the canopy to improve natural lighting, and the arrival of the intrusive motor cars, there has been little change. Dr E. Course

Southampton to Netley —
The Branch Line period

The route began with a four mile circuit, up to the bridge over the Itchen. This was determined by the choice of site for the bridge, and this in turn, fixed the point of the junction with the LSW main line. This was about one and a half miles from the terminus, and a new station was opened, immediately to the south of the junction. An earlier station had been opened in 1861, about a quarter of a mile further up the line and was named 'Portswood'. This was closed and the name transferred to the junction station opened with the new line, in 1866. (To avoid possible confusion with Portsmouth, the name of the junction station was changed to St Denys in 1876.) The choice of a junction facing Southampton depended on the estimate that most of the traffic would be coming from that place (including passengers from London who would change at the terminus rather than at St Denys). The station consisted of up and down platforms with a fine building in the Italianate style on the up side. Its main architectural features were repeated in the buildings provided at Woolston and Netley. A signal box adjoined the junction.

To reach the bridge the line curved sharply at twelve and a half chains radius and rose at 1 in 155. By the early 1860s suburban development had reached St Denys, and the line had to cross three streets between the junction and the river. Sixty-four houses, occupied by 209 persons 'of the labouring class' came within the limits of deviation but only five had to be demolished. Mr Galbraith, one of the engineers, stated that 'the persons so displaced will easily find accommodation of a similar character in the neighbourhood'.

Of the streets, Adelaide Road was crossed on the level and Ivy Road was stopped. An embankment carried the line up to the bridge and Priory Road, which bordered the river, was lowered by four feet to give a clearance of 13 feet under the railway.

The bridge itself was the main engineering work on the line. The site selected was the lowest point possible for making the crossing of the navigable River Itchen. The limit for vessels with fixed masts was Northam Bridge but the barges of the Itchen Navigation went on up to Winchester and needed to pass under the bridge at all states of the tide. Three wrought iron spans were erected at sufficient height to clear the barges. They were supported by solid abutments on each bank and by two pairs of cylindrical columns placed in the stream. These were made of cast iron filled with concrete to water level, topped up with masonry set in Portland cement. Contemporary accounts quote the cost of the bridge at between £14,500 and £15,000 — about a quarter of the contractor's price of £57,000 for constructing the whole line. Although it carried single track until 1910, with characteristic Victorian faith in the future, the bridge was constructed to take double track.

On the far side of the river, the line dropped at 1 in 80 to pass under the Northam Bridge company's road. (Both the Northam and Itchen Bridge companies owned their approach roads.) It was necessary to provide approach ramps for the overbridge, and a station was provided, 57 chains from St Denys. This was intended to appease the local landowners and the inhabitants of Bitterne for the deviation of the line away from the village. In its early days, it was referred to as 'Northam Road for Bitterne',

then 'Bitterne Road', and finally, in 1896, it became 'Bitterne'. It was always a 'second-class' station compared to Woolston and Netley, and this was reflected in its modest buildings. In fact the station house was so modest as to justify enlargement in 1902. The first road bridge consisted of an iron span, the road being raised about 14 feet to clear the railway.

Beyond Bitterne Station, the line ran down to the river bank which it followed as far as Woolston. The only constraint on this section was the obligation to provide access to the river for property that boarded the foreshore. As Woolston was approached, the line ran on to an embankment, climbing steeply at 1 in 90, before curving inland towards Netley. The attitude of the Itchen Bridge company towards the railway appears somewhat ambivalent, perhaps because such people as Thomas Chamberlayne were prominent in both undertakings. However, the Directors did express a fear that traffic from the developing area in and beyond Woolston, for destinations such as London, might use the new railway rather than cross by the floating bridge to reach the terminal station in Southampton. In the event, their fears were justified and there was a decline in the receipts of the bridge company. One of their hopes was that if a station was provided at Woolston, with convenient access to the bridge, passengers might prefer to cut across by the bridge rather than go four miles by the railway. With this in mind, the 1863 Act included a clause for the provision of a station to serve the bridge. ('The Company shall make and permanently maintain a Station on the Railway hereby authorised at or near the point marked Two Miles and one Furlong'). In fact, to facilitate construction,

Woolston Station was located at the point of transition between embankment and cutting at two miles and thirty two chains. There is no evidence of a great deal of interchange between the railway and the floating bridge at Woolston. Although the train took 15 minutes to go round by its circuitous route, and the floating bridge crossed in three or four minutes, this was hardly sufficient to encourage the effort required to transfer. However the ferry did offer greater frequency and lower fares. Above all, it started to operate much earlier in the mornings, and this, coupled to the growth of Woolston, meant that by the late 1860s, the bridge moved into its period of greatest prosperity.

Whether or not its role as an interchange point with the bridge had any significance, another impressive station building, comparable to those at St Denys and Netley, was provided at Woolston. It was placed on the up side with the booking office and waiting rooms on the ground floor, and accommodation for the station master above. An extensive forecourt gave access to the bridge company's approach road. The end of the cutting was widened on the down side, to make room for the goods yard.

Another clause in the 1863 Act stated that the railway 'must not interfere with the road between the Floating Bridge Terminal and the village of Itchen' and this accounts for the sharp curve with which the railway turns inland at Woolston. After the opening of the line, the LSWR Traffic Committee received a request for a station 'near Millers Pond' and it was decided that 'a temporary wooden box and platform be erected as an experiment'. This was opened, adjoining an overbridge, on 1st August 1866 and despite being little more than half a mile from Woolston must have justified itself. A brick

platform and a modest, single storey booking office and waiting room were provided. A house for the stationmaster was constructed on the nearby road. However, there was no goods yard, and like Bitterne, Sholing was rather a 'second class' station. The line reached its summit about a quarter of a mile beyond the station. Near this point, it ran out of the cutting on to an embankment which carried the line over the valley and the stream, below Millers Pond. Here a realignment of the Itchen Bridge Company's road avoided the need for a skewed bridge, but the embankment is pierced by a substantial three arch underbridge.

On the far side of the valley another cutting was entered and for about one and a half miles the line descended to its terminus at Netley. This was located just over half a mile from the Hospital and about half a mile from the nascent village. Part of an existing road became the station approach, road traffic being diverted over a bridge at the Southampton end of the station. The buildings were placed on the up side, and the line extended beyond the station on the alignment for Hamble Quay. However, it terminated at Hound Road and at this point, shortly after the opening of the line, a special platform was provided for the traffic of the Hospital.

The station was at a point of transition between cutting and embankment. However, the Hospital platform and the adjacent goods yard were on an embankment, rising above a steep sided valley.

The station building was in the same architectural style as St Denys and Woolston, but larger. It may well have been intended as a station fit for a queen, and it was so used on a number of occasions. For instance, on 29th November 1882 Queen Victoria arrived in the

Royal Train, which had come from Windsor via Basingstoke. A red carpet was laid on the platform and the waiting room was decorated with flowers and bunting.

However, this was a very special occasion. The service shown in Bradshaw for July 1866 shows eight stopping services in each direction, all calling at every station. In theory, the service could have been provided by 'one train in steam'. The fares to Bitterne (2d Single, Third Class) were the same as those to St Denys, reflecting the roundabout route of the railway and the possibility of passengers preferring to walk or ride over Northam Bridge. The first train left Southampton at 7.30am and Netley at 8.10am which was, of course, far too late to be of any use to the 'labouring classes'. On the other hand, third class accommodation was provided on all the trains. There were no through coaches, a change at Southampton being required. (For instance, the 8.10am from Netley connected with the 8.45am from Southampton to Waterloo). A typical train would have consisted of about half a dozen four-wheel compartment coaches and a brake van, hauled by a tank locomotive.

Top **The bridge over the River Itchen seen from the south in January 1973. The bridge was high enough to allow the passing of barges going up to Winchester, even at high tide. Although it now carries two electrified tracks, the appearance of the bridge has altered little since 1866.** Dr E. Course

Above **Netley station from the footbridge in December 1972. The original buildings at St Denys, Woolston and Netley were all constructed by Bulls and are virtually unchanged. However, since 1972 the platform seats have been replaced, as has the semaphore signal — the signal box has been removed to Ropley on the Mid Hants Railway.** Dr E. Course

Extension to Fareham and other developments

The financial crisis of 1866 caused a hiatus in railway promoting, but by 1873 there were signs of recovery. Plans deposited in 1873 and 1874 would have closed the gap between Netley and Fareham (for Portsmouth). The first line was to run from Fareham to Hillhead, where a pier was to be constructed for steamers to the Isle of Wight, and the second consisted of an extension from Hillhead to Netley, with the rather grandiose title of the 'Hants Coast Railway'. These failed to materialise, but among the items on the LSW (Various Powers) Act of 1882 was the long awaited extension from Netley to Fareham. The line, seven miles, six furlongs in length, was authorised in 1883, but not completed until 1889. From this date, most of the trains on the Netley line ran through between Southampton and Portsmouth, although a few trains — in 1899 two a day — continued to terminate at Netley. On the other hand, by 1896 through express trains between Portsmouth and Cardiff were using the Netley line.

In 1899 the junction at St Denys was moved from the London end to the Southampton end of the station, with new platforms provided for the Netley line. This would seem to have the advantage of enabling Netley line trains to be stopped in St Denys station, without fouling the main line. At this time, there were crossing places at Bitterne, Netley and Swanwick. An additional crossing place was added at Woolston in 1901, but subsequently the decision was taken to double the line throughout. This was not a major operation as land for double track had been acquired, and most bridges were constructed to take double track when the line was opened. The work was carried out in 1910 and 1911 and the opportunity was taken to rebuild the over-bridge adjoining Bitterne Station. (This was rebuilt again in 1932/1933 to accommodate increasing road traffic.) Rather more work was necessary at Sholing. Here the single track had passed through the centre of the overbridge adjoining the station. When the platform was constructed, instead of skewing the track, it was built with the end blocking one side of the bridge hole. It was necessary to demolish this platform, and to provide two new platforms, and also new station buildings. However, unlike the other three stations on the original line, Sholing was not provided with a signal box or goods yard.

In their 1884 (Various Powers) Bill the LSW included powers to construct a line from their yard at Netley towards the Hospital. It ended at the boundary of the War Department land, as presumably normal legislation was not required for government property. Nothing was done, and the provision of a waiting room on the existing Hospital platform in 1899 gave no indication of imminent development. Perhaps a clue is given by a piece in the *Southampton Times* of 23rd December 1899. It begins 'The railway from the Troop Siding at Netley to the Hospital which was suggested by the Queen on her last visit is about to be commenced. The acquisition of the necessary land has, thanks to Mr Tankerville Chamberlayne's patriotism, been much facilitated and during the week the way was staked out and levels taken'. The line was 48 chains (a little over half a mile) in length and for much of the way descended at a gradient of 1 in 80. (In fact, the ruling gradient was 1 in 68). It was constructed by the LSW on the authority of the General Manager and they were reimbursed by the W.D. Under the stimulus of the Boer War, construction proceeded rapidly. An LSW Notice of 11th April 1900 makes the point that the line was opened for the passing of Special Trains only. The W.D. built a platform, and later a shed for some ambulance coaches.

Having suggested the line, the Queen used it on 16th May 1900. The Royal Train started from the LSW station at Windsor, and travelled via Staines, Woking, Guildford and Fareham. Crimson cloth was laid on the platform and the Oxford Light Infantry provided a band and a guard of honour. The train left at 5.30pm and reached Windsor at 7.41pm. There is no mention of any problem in climbing the steep gradient but doubtlessly this was facilitated by having locomotives at both ends of the train, plus the presence of the Chairman and General Manager of the LSW, Sam Fay, the Traffic Superintendent and Dugald Drummond, the Locomotive Superintendent. The somewhat fulsome newspaper account finishes by stating that 'Truly, this must have been Netley Hospital Station's finest occasion'. Most hospital railways carried more coal and stores than people, but on account of its steep gradients, traffic on the Netley line was confined to ambulance trains. A trial with 20 coal trucks was made in October 1939 but not repeated. In the Second World War it was refurbished by the U.S. Army and received its greatest use in June and July 1944, carrying up to five 14 or 15 coach ambulance trains.

There were proposals to build an 18 inch gauge light railway to carry supplies from Netley to the training ship 'Mercury', moored off Hamble. This was not constructed, although a narrow gauge railway did operate in 'Mercury's' shore establishment. Oddly enough, the waterfront at Hamble was finally reached by a standard gauge line in 1918. This was built for a seaplane base, but was later acquired and operated to serve an oil depot. The junction was not on the original Netley line, but on the extension to Fareham, about half a mile beyond Netley.

A line that might have produced considerable traffic was never built. In 1909, about one and a half miles of railway was authorised from a point about half a mile beyond Sholing station down to the foreshore at Woolston. The LSWR acquired Southampton Docks in 1892 and, aided by the increase in size of transatlantic liners had persuaded the White Star line to move from Liverpool to Southampton. One of White Star's requirements was dry dock accommodation and rather than build a larger dry dock alongside their Trafalgar Dock of 1905, the LSWR decided to develop a new site at Woolston. The proposed dry dock would have been large enough to take any vessel that was likely to be constructed, its length being 1600 feet with a width of 115 feet. (After a period with the Floating Dry Dock of 1924, the Southern Railway built the King George V Dry Dock of 1933 to take the Queens, with a length of 1200 feet and a width of 135 feet.) Despite a number of advantages of the Woolston site, development was concentrated on the Southampton side and after the Second World War, the land purchased for the railway to serve it was sold to Southampton Corporation for less than it had cost the railway company.

The extension to the hospital was opened in 1900. Wartime conditions may have led to haste, reflected in the shallowness of the cutting, which gave a ruling gradient of 1 in 68. The view shows the cutting in December 1972, after the removal of the track but before the growth of vegetation. Dr E. Course

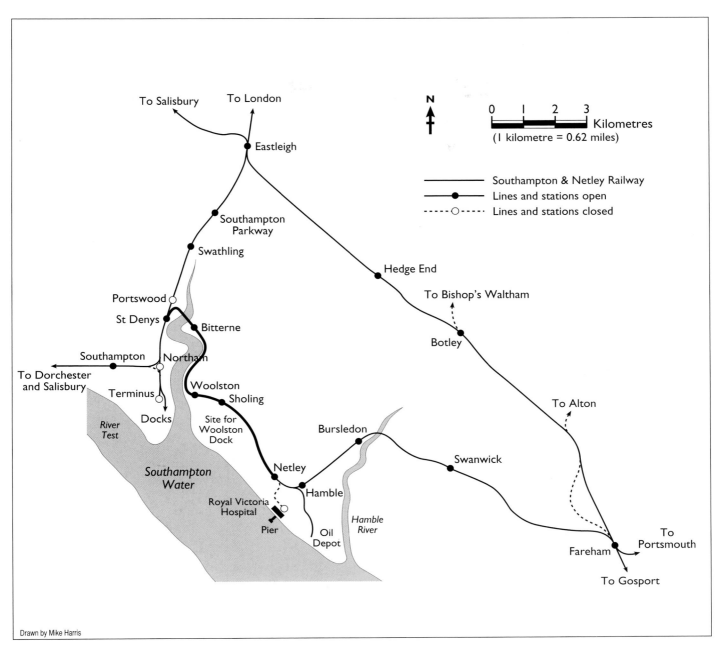

Drawn by Mike Harris

A stopping train from Southampton to Portsmouth running into Bitterne on 12th June 1957. Detail changes since have included the demolition of the signal box and the reduction of passenger accommodation to standard NSE shelters. Electricity has replaced gas lighting, and the station building has been leased. The main 'period' feature is the train, consisting of T9 class No.30729, built by Dubs in 1900, hauling LSW compartment coaches.

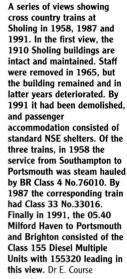

A series of views showing cross country trains at Sholing in 1958, 1987 and 1991. In the first view, the 1910 Sholing buildings are intact and maintained. Staff were removed in 1965, but the building remained and in latter years deteriorated. By 1991 it had been demolished, and passenger accommodation consisted of standard NSE shelters. Of the three trains, in 1958 the service from Southampton to Portsmouth was steam hauled by BR Class 4 No.76010. By 1987 the corresponding train had Class 33 No.33016. Finally in 1991, the 05.40 Milford Haven to Portsmouth and Brighton consisted of the Class 155 Diesel Multiple Units with 155320 leading in this view. Dr E. Course

The Southampton and Netley Railway today
By 1994, the Southampton and Netley had been modernised with resignalling, electrification and a remarkable upsurge in through passenger services. On the negative side, all the goods yards and the Hospital branch had been abandoned.

Starting at Adelaide Road crossing, the signal box of 1910, after acting as a crossing box with full lifting barriers from 1966, was demolished within a week of the resignalling of St Denys in October 1981. The crossing is now protected by half barriers, observed by Closed Circuit Television, and operated from the Eastleigh Panel Box. At Bitterne the goods yard was closed in 1959 and the signal box in 1966. The plain station house survives but not in railway use; passenger accommodation consists of standard Network SouthEast shelters. The fine station building

of 1866 at Woolston is Listed Grade II, and although not all of it is in railway use, it is well maintained. The signal box was closed as part of Phase One of the Southampton Resignalling Scheme in March 1980, and the traditional semaphore signals replaced by coloured light signals. However, the box itself is the only survivor on the Netley line, being preserved and rented by the Solent Model Railway Society. A minor change has been the replacement of the gas by electric lighting in 1968 (this was done at all the Netley line stations). Gone without a trace has been the extensive goods yard. At its peak, this had a goods shed containing a crane of two tons capacity and a 10 ton crane outside. It was closed to general traffic in 1966 but continued in use for non-rail commercial activities, including the distribution of coal and oil products until 1985. At this

time, the various businesses were removed and about 40 houses were crammed on to the site.

Sholing lost its staff in 1965, although for a while railway tickets could be obtained from a nearby newsagent. The buildings of 1910 were attacked by vandals and had deteriorated greatly before their demolition in 1990. They were replaced by standard Network SouthEast shelters. The only public road level crossing on the Netley line was at Adelaide Road in St Denys, but other crossings included that for a footpath at Keepers Bottom. (This was advocated as a possible site for a halt by the local council in 1906). Particularly after electrification, the crossing was considered dangerous and it has now been closed. At Netley, a major change was the closure of the goods yard in 1962 and now most of the site is occupied by

commercial undertakings. The signal box was closed in March 1980, in connection with Phase One of the Southampton Resignalling Scheme. A brief record of it working was made by a film unit from the University of Southampton before its removal to the Mid-Hants Railway at Ropley. The station building of 1866, like Woolston, is Listed Grade II, and is very well maintained. It is hoped that it may become a restaurant, with unique rail access. In contrast, almost nothing remains of the Hospital branch. The last train ran down it in 1955, and long before its formal abandonment in 1963 it had become overgrown. Demolition began on the Hospital site in 1955 with the removal of the pier. The main buildings and the station were demolished in 1967. The site now forms the Royal Victoria Country Park of the Hampshire County Council, who also maintain the

'Royal Chapel', which once formed a central feature of the vast building, as a memorial to the Hospital, its soldiers, nurses and patients. The original objective of the Southampton and Netley Railway has gone.

In contrast, whilst no new stations have been opened, the four stations of 1866 all remain open to passenger traffic. There was a great improvement in the local services in 1957 when diesel trains were introduced. For instance, Netley, which had eight departures in each direction in 1866 and 19 in 1947, by 1966 had 36. At the same time, through cross country services had sunk to one train a day between Cardiff and Portsmouth. In 1994, it is this cross country route, now operated by the diesel trains of Regional Railways, which shows the most dramatic improvement. Instead of the one train of 1966, there are now 17 running between Brighton or Portsmouth

and Bristol and South Wales. However, they use the Netley line but do not serve its stations, running non-stop between Southampton and Fareham. With electrification came a new service from Southampton to London Victoria via the Netley line, the Sussex Coast and Gatwick Airport. Like the cross-country services, these trains do not serve local stations. Between Southampton and Fareham they call only at Swanwick. In fact, the local service has declined from its peak in the early days of dieselisation, and now consists of a basic hourly service between Southampton and Portsmouth. For instance, Netley now has 17 departures.

The Southampton and Netley began as a local branch line and now flourishes as part of various through routes. Its future is assured by carrying traffic which would not have entered the minds of its promoters.

By Rail from the Two Barnets

George Wilmot

With the story of commuting from New Barnet and High Barnet, Professor Wilmot develops the theory that 'rapid transit' type of operation, while suited to central areas, is inappropriate for outer suburban work.

Who has the more comfortable, less stressful and preferable journey, the rail traveller from New Barnet or from High Barnet? There was little difference from 1872 when the railway reached High Barnet; though New Barnet, on the main line of the Great Northern Railway, had a slight edge. But in 1940 when the High Barnet branch was transferred from the LNER to the Northern Line of the London Transport tube system, High Barnet gained a very clear advantage. This continued for 20 years, but troubles began to emerge on the Northern Line by the end of the 1950s. Electrification in 1976-7 completed a swing back to New Barnet.

Why is this? Both locations are more or less the same distance from inner London. New Barnet via Finsbury Park to Kings Cross is 14.7 kms (9.15 miles) and to Moorgate 16.4 kms (10.2 miles). High Barnet via Camden Town to Charing Cross is 17.5 kms (10.87 miles), and to Moorgate 20.7 kms (12.86 miles). To discover the answer, a fascinating story unravels over the last century. It shows clearly how apparently sensible planning can go sadly awry. In doing so it can advance lessons for the future of London's transport as it faces such a critical time at the beginning of the 21st century.

Confusion can be caused by the multiplicity of places labelled Barnet. The earliest grew up in the eighth century round a hill-top traversed by the original Great North Road. The prefix 'Chipping' (a market) was added. Later East Barnet grew up on lower ground, two miles to the south east. Still further medieval expansion saw Friern Barnet established four miles to the south and like Chipping Barnet, on the Great North Road. With the coming of the GNR in 1850, when a somewhat imposing station was built in the valley two miles east of Chipping Barnet and on the road thence to East Barnet, the new settlement of New Barnet developed. It grew rapidly during the middle and late Victorian periods.

When the GNR eventually arrived at Chipping Barnet from Finchley in 1872, the terminus was named High Barnet. This then became the normal prefix for what was Chipping Barnet. (The new London Borough of Barnet, incorporated in 1965, revived 'Chipping' and petitioned London Transport to change the name. This was refused because of the cost of changing many hundreds of maps, diagrams and notices.)

Facing Page Upper **Stanier 2-6-2T No.79 en route from Broad Street, in charge of elderly non-corridor coaches.** Lens of Sutton

Facing Page Lower **When LT tube trains reached High Barnet it was a great step forward, but the Great Northern station was not rebuilt.** LT Museum U58679

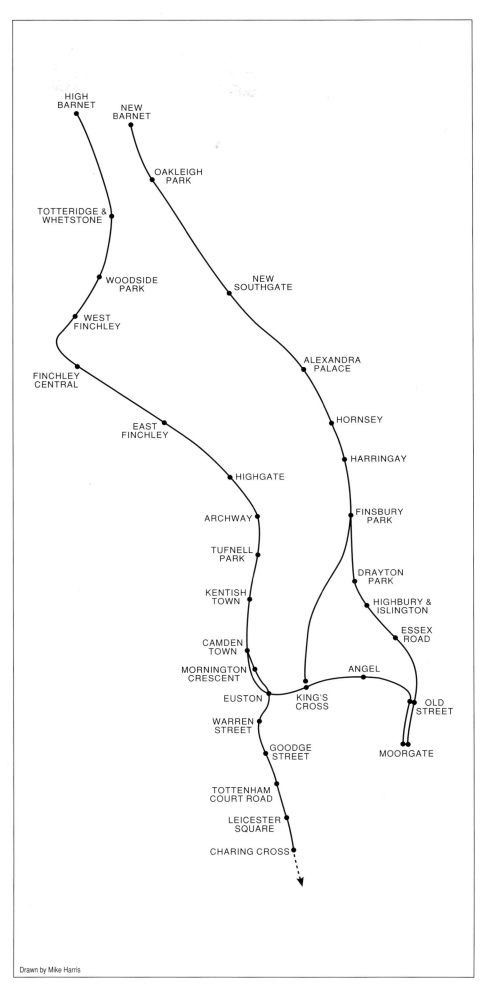

Drawn by Mike Harris

A typical LNER suburban train. A train for New Barnet approaches Harringay. It is all-Gresley: two 'quad-art' sets are headed by N2 0-6-2T No.4725. Lens of Sutton

The coming of the GNR to Chipping Barnet
It was topography which relegated Chipping Barnet, situated on a hill, to branch line status, leaving New Barnet on the main line along the valley. The GNR did not follow the established line of the Great North Road, which climbed up to Highgate and thence traversed the high ground to Chipping Barnet, but made an easterly detour up the valley of Pymme's Brook to Potters Bar. Chipping Barnet declined badly, having lost its function as the first staging post on the Great North Road. 'The road is finished and all trade has moved down the valley to New Barnet' bemoaned an observer in 1860.

By the 1860s more determined efforts to scale the Northern Heights were being made, an earlier 1845 proposal having come to nothing. An Edgware Highgate & London (EH&L) Railway Bill of 1861 made some progress before failing. It laid the basis for the simpler and successful Act of 3rd June 1862. The line agreed became the BR line, now closed, from Finsbury Park to Highgate Wood Sidings, the LT line from Highgate to Mill Hill East, and the now lifted section on to Edgware.

The EH&L struggled financially as the 1860s advanced. Landslips between Finsbury Park and Highgate and the cost of the large brick viaduct over the Dollis Brook caused budgets to go awry. To make matters worse, the EH&L found itself in the middle of the row between the GNR and the Midland which led to the latter opening its extension from Bedford to St Pancras, completed in 1868.

The new Midland line cut across the EH&L at Mill Hill and gave a much quicker route to London. The EH&L looked for another outlet, and focussed attention on Chipping Barnet through a short branch from Finchley. The Midland promoted a line from Cricklewood to Finchley connecting with the EH&L and then following the east side of the road to Chipping Barnet. The EH&L proposal, the existing line, is on the west side. For reasons difficult to understand the GNR promoted a third line, which was to be much further west with a Chipping Barnet station north of the present one. From thence the GNR also sought powers to join the main line north of Hadley Wood station, involving a steep tunnel under Hadley Green.

In practice the GNR now held the EH&L as a puppet company. They were to work it and receive half the receipts and had subscribed up to one third of the £220,000 capital. They also had the right to appoint three of the eight directors on the EH&L Board. So why promote another line? The only possible reason was that the GNR considered it better to have two plans to put forward against the Midland's one.

In the event the EH&L's plan won the day and received the Royal Assent on 16th July 1866. Crippling debts resulted in the GNR acquiring the company exactly a year later. The single line to Edgware was opened on 22nd August 1867 and doubling to Finchley approved in January 1868. The construction of the line to Chipping Barnet proceeded at a very leisurely pace and was not opened until Monday 1st April 1872 to 'High Barnet' station. Although termed a branch line, the pattern of services showed it was the main arm, as the traffic on the Edgware line was badly reduced by the Midland. Chipping Barnet was now connected to the railway, and began to re-establish its former importance.

The Suburban 'Incubus' — A storm in a teacup?

The minutes of the GNR's Traffic and Ways & Works Committee reveal a complete lack of appreciation of the likely problems arising from suburban commuter traffic. It was regarded as subsidiary to the long distance passenger and coal traffic, and as a useful contribution to the railway's fixed costs. The GNR simply did not appreciate that the concept of living and working in different places would become normal. There was little effort to provide even elementary facilities for passengers. Seven Sisters Road (now Finsbury Park) had no waiting room until 1869. This was agreed at a shareholder's meeting, when one of them declared that 'Seven Sisters Road has become an incubus'. The word became applied to the whole pattern of GNR suburban traffic and is given great play by Grinling in his *History of the Great Northern Railway* (1904).

Was the suburban traffic as bad as the GNR made out? A dictionary defines 'incubus' as an 'evil spirit' or 'nightmare'. After all the GNR commuter traffic was only a trickle compared with the lines south of the Thames and into Liverpool Street. But all these railways were geared to this traffic as their main business. The GNR always reacted after the crisis was upon them. A classic example was the hurried negotiations with the North London to gain access to Broad Street which would give the GNR a second City terminus to relieve the crowded Widened Lines to Moorgate. Unfortunately in its haste to complete in February 1875, the GNR allowed North London trains to all suburban points north of Finsbury Park, resulting in additional congestion there.

For the Barnets the service was much the same from 1872 to 1914. The off-peak service was good but the peak hours tended to suffer delays and there were frequent scrambles at Finsbury Park to change trains. In December 1890 the opening of the City & South London Tube was of no direct consequence, yet it was eventually to have far reaching significance.

The London Underground and the 1920s expansion

The 1906 Report of the Royal Commission on London Traffic was probably the best ever produced on this subject. The Commissioners had remarkable perception. While most of their recommendations were abandoned in the short term, they were revived nearly a century later. They strongly advocated Parliamentary support for the new tube lines as, in view of severe surface congestion in the urban area, they felt the only solution was to transfer some traffic underground. Their recommendations for tube lines only applied to the central rather than suburban areas, and they urged short shuttle services with no junctions.

Among the new Tube railways, the Great Northern, Piccadilly & Brompton (later to become the Piccadilly Line) was originally planned in part as a relief line for the GNR between Wood Green (now Alexandra Park) and Aldwych. It was not taken very seriously by the GNR, whose main flow of commuters was to the City. By the first decade of the century, also, the West End had not developed its present office functions.

The Charing Cross, Euston & Hampstead differed from its companion lines. It was taken out of its urban context and developed suburban functions by planned extensions, by the 1899 Act to extend to the summit community of Highgate, and by the American C.T. Yerkes to continue beyond the Northern Heights to Golders Green. These extensions involved a junction at Camden Town.

These developments would have seemed very remote to the commuters from the Barnets. But by 1907 the C&SL had been extended northward to Moorgate and thence to Kings Cross and Euston, where there was a relatively easy interchange with the CXE&H at the higher level. Connection with the CXE&H at Camden Town was completed in 1924. Southward, the line had ventured into suburban traffic and reached Morden in 1926. In that year a connection at Kennington was made with the CXE&H. In 1924 the extension to Edgware was completed and the title of Northern Line was adopted in 1937.

The LNER drags its feet and finds Salvation in 1935

At the end of World War I railways in Great Britain were run down and poorly equipped to face the rapidly changing transport demand. The solution of the 1921 Act was a compromise between public ownership and the preservation of private railway competition. Of the four companies then formed, the London & North Eastern Railway had the most difficult ground to plough, inheriting an almost impossible network to weld into one coherent system. The LNER concentrated its efforts on the coalfields and long-distance passengers. Improvement of commuter services from either of the Barnets was scarcely a priority matter and steam traction remained the order of the day. Even the articulated stock replacing the obsolete GNR's lacked the comfort of contemporary Southern electric, while the LMSR trains from Broad Street were a disgrace until 1933 when the old NLR stock was replaced by LMS-built bogie stock. The latter vehicles were quite luxurious for the period.

Above **LMS trains from Broad Street were interspersed with the LNER ones and serving the same destinations. Here a 'Jinty' Class 3 0-6-0T heads a train of LMS non-corridors. Four wheelers were in use until the early 1930s.** Lens of Sutton

Great Northern architecture on the High Barnet line is largely intact at the northern end. This view is of Woodside Park station. LT Museum U58677

The 1925 North and North East London Traffic Inquiry censured the LNER for 'exhibiting a want of consideration for the needs of suburban traffic which the travelling public ... feel they are entitled to expect'. The 1929 Development (Loan Guarantees and Grants) Act gave the Company an opportunity to submit an application for assistance towards electrification of some of its suburban services, including those affecting the two Barnets.

The Government was now however looking at the possibility of setting up the London Passenger Transport Board and informed the LNER that if this was done, the scheme would be submitted to the Joint Traffic Committee (of main line railways and London Transport). This was eventually done and in 1935 its plan was formulated. This included electrification from Finsbury Park to High Barnet, Edgware and the short branch from Highgate to Alexandra Palace and extension of the tube from Archway to East Finchley to join the former GNR line. As a result the short shuttle, mass transit role of the tubes, as envisaged by the 1906 Commissioners, was completely abandoned, not for the first time. As far as the Northern Line was concerned, the system would be unduly complex and transits long. A proposal to link the former GNR main line suburban services to the tube system was abandoned on the grounds of cost and operating problems. After this the LNER never returned to its proposals to electrify the main line and left the New Barnet commuters condemned to an ancient system.

1940-1959: High Barnet in the Tube System
East Finchley was linked to the tube system on 3rd July 1939, and High Barnet on 14th April 1940. At first trains ran only via Charing Cross; but through running via Bank began in 1941. The Edgware line was only electrified as far as Mill Hill East (from 19th May 1941). From High Barnet to Morden is 34 kms (21 miles) via Charing Cross and nearly three kilometres further via Bank, in contrast with the 7 kms (4.2 miles) of the original CXE&H.

In June 1946 London Transport announced that the planned electrification from Mill Hill East to Edgware and of the Alexandra Palace branch line would resume. Meanwhile New Barnet remained with a somewhat infrequent steam service (three per hour each to Moorgate and Kings Cross) though commuters living east of New Barnet had, since 1933, been able to use buses to reach the Piccadilly extension via Enfield West (Oakwood), an inconvenient option for most, however.

In 1949 a London Plan Working Party stated that tube lines over 19-22.5 kms (12-14 miles) were too long, an echo of the 1906 sentiment. But little notice was taken. The Northern Line extension to Edgware and the proposed new line thence to Bushey Heath were however abandoned in February 1954. Plans to electrify from Finsbury Park to Alexandra Palace and to Highgate via Crouch End were also dropped, the emaciated steam service to Alexandra Palace being withdrawn after 3rd July 1954 in a dramatic reversal of its fortune.

The problem with the Northern Line stemmed from the two junctions at Camden Town and Kennington. In running a highly intensive service, the junction at Camden Town worked smoothly provided every train was in its correct path, otherwise complications ensued. It has not been until recent years that computer-assisted control of the junctions has been provided, overcoming some of the operational difficulties at these two locations.

Suburban growth led to continuous increase in passenger traffic from High Barnet throughout the 1950s. It was mostly geared to the West End, adding pressure on the Charing Cross Line. Largely because of trade union refusal to allow longer off-peak trains during the 1958 bus strike, the line was unable to cope. In January 1959 passenger resistance reached breaking point and there was a recurrence of 'stay in strikes', the first of which was at Golders Green in 1909. On one service passengers were ordered to leave a High Barnet train at East Finchley. Commuters had already had long delays, being detrained at Camden Town and Archway, and this was the last straw. Most refused to leave until the appearance of the Transport Police 30 minutes later. An identical incident occurred in 1989. On both occasions there was a clash of view between the operators and those responsible for giving a service to passengers. The former were concerned to restore trains to their correct path as soon as possible. But communication between the control centre and station staff was weak and tempers became frayed.

The upheaval of conversion. Steam and electricity at Finchley Central in 1939. Note the Great Northern station buildings, which will be swept away to accommodate the southbound island platform. LT Museum

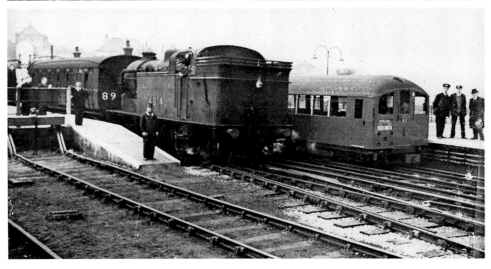

The last days of regular steam operation at High Barnet. A special train of 1938 tube stock stands alongside. The introduction of electric trains brought an increase in frequency on the Barnet branch from eight trains per hour in the peaks to fourteen. Travelling time from High Barnet to King's Cross (calling at all stations) reduced from 33 minutes to 28. Capital Transport

Electrification for New Barnet at Last

On the New Barnet line steam was gradually replaced by diesel multiple units, a process completed by 1965. The latter gave a more frequent service and performed reasonably well. There are nostalgic memories of friendly and helpful platform staff (virtually unknown at High Barnet) and waiting rooms with coal fires in winter. There was even a night service of hourly trains, the best in the country, which lasted until 1988.

The suburban electrification so confidently predicted by Grinling eventually came about. The 1955 Modernisation plan envisaged it as part of the East Coast Main Line conversion. But it was not until 1971 that suburban electrification was considered eligible for a grant under the 1968 Transport Act. On 8th November 1976 a 20-minute off-peak service was inaugurated between Welwyn Garden City and Moorgate calling at all stations. Unfortunately, in its early years, it acquired a reputation for unreliability caused by technical and labour-relations difficulties.

In later years the service was reduced to half hourly and diverted to Kings Cross in the evenings and at weekends. But when they settled down, the Class 313 units proved to be much superior to tube stock in terms of comfort, riding qualities and speed. The balance had tipped fairly decisively, except for service frequency, to New Barnet.

The Author wishes to thank Alan A. Jackson, John Aylard, and H.P. White for assistance.

Above **N2 69588 heads a train from Moorgate at New Barnet in April 1959. Four trains per hour each ran between New Barnet and King's Cross and Moorgate at this time. The numbers in 1994 are two and five respectively.** John Aylard

Left **Game, set and match for New Barnet. A Class 313 EMU at King's Cross on a working from Welwyn Garden City via New Barnet in 1981. These units are far better suited to suburban services than tube stock.** A.C. Mott

Bexhill's Lost Route to London

Alan A. Jackson

The Bexhill West branch received brief mention in the Summer 1993 (Vol. 3 No.4) RSE article on the Hastings main line ('1066 and All That'). Alan A. Jackson now looks at the history of this unlucky line in detail.

Whatever radical changes our present Conservative Government's highly controversial scheme to privatise and break up British Rail may bring, it seems unlikely indeed that it will result in the construction of new railways to compete with existing services, even if this is a logical consequence of the political dogma that lies behind it. That this extreme result of a 'free market' situation in rail transport was still a possibility in Britain as recently as the beginning of the 20th century is demonstrated by the opening of a second and very costly railway to Bexhill in 1902. This was however to be the last truly 'competitive' line built in the south east and it is interesting that it survived for less than the average human lifespan.

The London Brighton & South Coast Railway (LB&SCR) had served Bexhill as early as June 1846, when the opening of the section from Lewes to St Leonards completed the present route from the town to London via Keymer Junction and the Brighton main line. The LB&SCR was to enjoy over 50 years of private monopoly here. Its nearest neighbour was of course the South Eastern Railway (SER), which had reached Hastings via Tunbridge Wells in 1851 and, after some initial recalcitrance, admitted LB&SCR trains to Hastings via a connection at Bopeep Junction, just over three miles east of Bexhill.

A branch to Bexhill off the SER's 1852 Hastings line, from a point just south of Battle had been proposed as early as 1862 but

in the 1880s there was a more purposeful stirring of interest, prompted by the beginnings of Bexhill's development as a seaside resort and a desire to remedy its perceived disadvantages in rail communication with London compared with its rivals, St Leonards and Hastings. There were proposals in 1884 (the Bexhill Direct Railway), 1885 and 1889, the latter associated with the contractors Lucas & Aird. However, as so often the case, a purposeful personality was needed to get the scheme off the ground and such a man was about to appear. In 1894 Henry Cosmo Orme Bonsor secured a seat on the SER board, becoming deputy chairman in 1895 and chairman in 1898. The old men and the old inertia were on the way out and Bonsor, a shrewd and successful businessman, a director of the Bank of England and MP for Surrey North East, was to put new life into the SER and within a short time would secure a joint working agreement with its longtime rival, the London, Chatham & Dover Railway.

It seems very likely that Bonsor was a principal motivator of the next scheme to serve Bexhill off the SER Hastings main line, the nominally independent Crowhurst, Sidley & Bexhill Railway, promoted in 1896 with a proposed capital of £180,000, a high figure for a mere 4½ miles of line. He was certainly on the board of the new company, as were the SER's ageing chairman Sir George Russell and another SER director. Despite this strong whiff of patronage by a major competitor, which must have discomfited the LB&SCR, the bill had a successful passage through parliament. In 1897 J. Price (Messrs Price & Reeves) was appointed contractor and the SER advanced a substantial loan, enabling work to start at the turn of the year. The engineer was Arthur Barrie. A second Act of 1st July 1898 authorised further capital, partly for expensive land acquisition at Bexhill, and also some deviations at the Bexhill end. Earl de la Warr, who was largely responsible for the modern development of Bexhill as a 'select' seaside resort, expressed considerable interest in the new railway. He sought an invitation to join its board, and was admitted, becoming chairman, in 1899. The company remained separate from its patron and protector until 1st January 1907.

Construction was difficult and costly, involving as it did some substantial engineering works. The branch left the SER at Crowhurst, where that company provided a new station just north of the junction. This had a pair of central through roads, two side platforms on loops from the main lines and an up and down bay into each platform at the country end for the branch trains. The up bay had an engine release road. Two signal boxes served the new layout and passenger and staff accommodation was in red and yellow brick buildings under tiled hipped roofs, although there was no shelter over most of the long platforms. A long approach road and a Station Hotel were also financed by the SER.

The principal engineering feature of the new line was the quarter-mile long viaduct carrying the tracks up to 67ft over the very soggy Combe Haven Valley just south of Crowhurst. This structure, which was to become known locally as the '17 Arches', took nearly two years to build and was not completed until autumn 1900. The problem lay in the treacherous subsoil of peat and soft sandy clays separated from underlying hard blue clay by a bed of shingle. After finding that piles driven into the ground would not form a stable base for the piers, the engineers used large concrete blocks as foundations. During construction there were several subsidences in the embankments at either end and a serious landslip occurred at the northern approach in the mid 1920s. Some nine million blue Staffordshire and red bricks were required.

THE CROWHURST, SIDLEY & BEXHILL RAILWAY

Scale approx 2ins to 1 mile

The arrow indicates the Combe Haven Viaduct

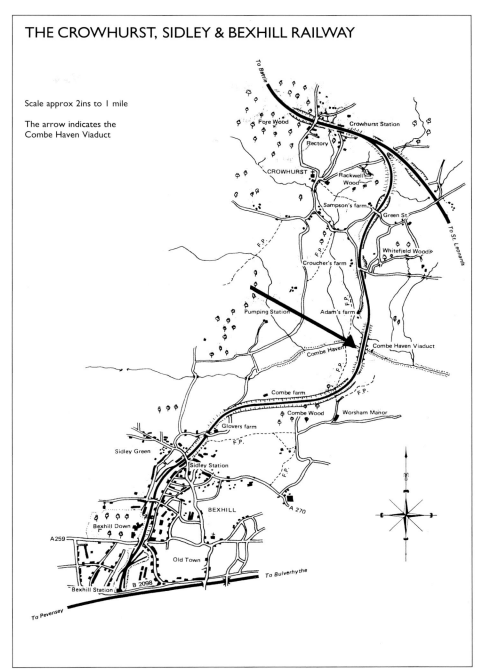

The frontage of Bexhill West station while still in use in 1954. The building is now used by Fryer's Auction Galleries. R.C. Riley

For reasons that are not entirely clear from surviving records, the station buildings on the double track branch bordered on the extravagant, in great contrast to the normal spartan standards of the SER. The spacious terminus, on low-lying land on the western edge of Bexhill, was much enhanced by a very handsome building placed across the end of the line. This had a decorated central entrance arch and two prominent gables either side of it. A fine moulded pediment adorned the arch but the decoration was cemented over and pebble-dashed in later years. Faced with red brick and Bath stone dressing with Welsh slate roof this frontage block was served by the new Terminus Road and it was given further dignity by what *The Railway Magazine* described as an 'artistic' clock tower under a small cupola. Within was a lofty beamed-ceilinged entrance hall warmed from a vast fireplace, the ticket and parcels office, the stationmaster's and inspector's offices and ladies' and general waiting rooms. A smaller block, placed at right angles at the eastern end, also decorated with a pretty cupola at its centre, housed a 32ft by 30ft refreshment room managed by Spiers & Pond, porters' and lamp rooms and men's lavatories. After closure of the line, this second building was converted to a public house called *The Rother Arms*.

Of the two island platforms, each 700ft in length and 30ft wide, the easternmost (nos. 1 and 2) was protected for 400ft by glazed lattice girder canopies, as was the 40ft by 90ft concourse behind the buffer stops. The canopied area was paved, the exposed section gravelled. At the easternmost platform face were two tracks, the second an engine run-round road, but there were three tracks between the other two faces, including a central engine release road. What would

have been platform 4 had no track alongside and platform 3 very quickly fell into disuse for passenger purposes. The whole unfinished and uncanopied area of platforms 3 and 4 was then left to grow wild grass in later years. Gas lighting was adopted for the platforms and the signal lamps; although there was electric light in the station buildings from the opening it was never extended to the rest of the complex.

Provision for freight traffic matched the extravagance of the optimistic passenger facilities. The yard, on the east side, had a large goods shed, three cranes, five cattle stalls and three road vehicle loading docks. Road access was from an entrance opposite the York Hotel in Lower Station Road. At first, business was sufficient to keep a shunting locomotive more or less busy for much of the day but after World War 1 freight workings fell to two daily and finally only one, usually worked by a Bulleid 'Q1' 0-6-0 out from and returning to Tonbridge yard.

To the west of the passenger terminus and running lines were four carriage sidings and a two-road locomotive shed, 119ft by 32ft, with coal stage and a 54ft 9in turntable. Water for the tank here came along the line from Combe Haven in pipes laid by Price under the original contract. A sub shed of Hastings and, from 1929, of St Leonards in SR and BR days, this building, which could accommodate four tank locos, was sold to Hall & Co in 1938 for use as a warehouse. It still survives.

Little restraint was shown in provision of signalling equipment ordered from Evans, O'Donnell & Co. for here and the rest of the new line. The Yard Box had 123 levers (80 working) and the Station Box, unusually placed across the buffer stop ends of platforms 2 and 3, had 22 (12 working). By about

1914 this small box was reduced to a ground frame but the building survived intact until closure of the line.

Sidley, the only intermediate station, served the old village of Sidley Green, to the west of the line, then on the point of expanding south eastwards to become a northern suburb of the seaside resort. Here the road level building was in similar style and materials to Bexhill on a much smaller scale. An hotel was built opposite by the railway company. In the cutting below, the two side platforms which extended to 490ft, were graced by artistic wooden waiting sheds. At the Bexhill end, west of the line, there was a freight yard with goods shed and a 20-lever signal box with 16 working levers. The ticket office at road level was closed in 1938 as an economy and replaced by one in the up side waiting shed which allowed the station to be single-manned. Both Sidley and Bexhill stations were built to the designs of Messrs Barry & Mercer.

Leaving Crowhurst, the line descended at 1 in 90 and 1 in 100 to the viaduct, then climbing on the other side of the valley at 1 in 170. There were no other significant gradients but the line fell 126ft between Crowhurst and its coastal terminus. The soil removed by steam navvies from the cutting east of Sidley was used for the embankments and also to create a level site for the Bexhill facilities.

After a formal opening ceremony on 31st May 1902, with the usual flag decorations, public services, including the new station at Crowhurst junction, were available from Sunday, 1st June. Bexhill was now 62 miles from London (Charing Cross) against the 71¾ to London (Victoria) via Keymer Junction (78 via Eastbourne). This improvement was at first exploited. Through coaches were attached and detached from the

Freight was always a minor activity on the branch and a daily service from Tonbridge sufficed in later years. On 15th December 1949 Q1 0-6-0 leaves Sidley on the return working to Tonbridge. Note the goods shed. S.C. Nash

main line trains at Crowhurst, two to Victoria and two from that terminus (the journeys taking 108 minutes each way) and also two Up and one Down from Charing Cross. Better still was one through train daily to and from London timed at 99min in contrast to the two hours or more via the LB&SCR. Conscious of the threat, the LB&SCR arranged for a rebuilding of its Bexhill station on a more spacious and commodious scale, whilst still using only two platforms; this work was completed in 1902.

The initial competitive attitude was not sustained; enthusiasm for poaching the rival's passengers was presumably tempered by lack of success. Despite the very rapid development of the town between 1880 and 1900, its largely middle class residents and visitors, conservative in their behaviour, remained loyal to the LB&SCR. Further damage to the line's health was inflicted in the Great War. In response to a directive from the Railway Executive Committee for cuts in passenger train services from 1st January 1917 to release locomotives, stock and men for war purposes, the SE&CR produced a long list which included the total closure of the Bexhill branch. Working of public coal and military freight was resumed on 5th November 1917 and curiously, two passenger services each way were restored on *Tuesdays and Fridays only* from late 1917. This was 'largely for the convenience of visitors at Bexhill who desire to visit Battle Abbey', according to *The Railway & Travel Monthly*. Full daily services were not available again until 1st March 1919 and Sidley did not reopen to passengers until 14th June the following year. This lack of urgency in restoring peacetime services vividly demonstrates the SE&CR's perception at this period of the value of its Bexhill white elephant.

The interior of Bexhill West No.1 signal box in 1950. Its size reflects the over-lavish provision of facilities. J.J. Smith

Between 27th November 1949 and 5th June 1950 Bo-Peep tunnel between West St Leonards and Warrior Square was closed for repairs and all Hastings trains were diverted to Bexhill West. On 29th May the 12.25 from Charing Cross headed by Schools Class 4-4-0 No.30921 *Shrewsbury* pauses at Sidley. Note the Pullman buffet car. J.J. Smith

Crowhurst station on 25th July 1953 looking towards Tonbridge. Rebuilt Wainwright 4-4-0 No.31783 brings in a down Hastings train. Schedules required two pull and push trains at certain times to work the Bexhill Branch. In the down side bay H 0-4-4T No.31274 powers the connection. R.C. Riley

After Grouping in 1923 it became necessary to distinguish the two stations now in the same ownership. The former LB&SCR premises became Bexhill Central from 9th July 1923 and the other Bexhill was dubbed Bexhill West, but not until November 1929. Justifiable adoption of the term Central may have enticed some incoming strangers away from the branch but for some years after the Grouping an attempt seems to have been made to improve the services at the West station and divert the London traffic to this route. After interruption in World War 1,

through trains to London were restored in 1919 and in the early 1920s the morning businessmen's train reached Cannon Street in only 95 minutes, using the through lines at Crowhurst. At first the SR arranged for most Hastings via Tonbridge trains to include three corridor coaches for Bexhill West. In 1930 there were 19 leaving from Crowhurst Mondays to Fridays with two late night connections on Wednesdays and in summer a number of extras on Saturdays for holidaymakers. Of the 19, 11 were through Bexhill West portions from London-Hastings trains.

But even before its electrification, as has been suggested already, many remained loyal to the old LB&SCR services, preferring the more central situation of the Bexhill station and the total avoidance of any necessity to change trains. There was almost certainly a loss of business at Bexhill West following the electrification of the former LBSCR route in 1935, not because the electrics were any faster (all went in and out of Eastbourne and took a tedious 106-108 minutes to reach London) but the basic service was better than the steam trains via Crowhurst, with trains every hour all with refreshment facilities and extra workings at peak hours. Certainly the SR was in no doubt from this time which was the 'main route' and the Bexhill West services were allowed to deteriorate from the late 1930s. Push-pulls restricted to the branch replaced some of the through coach workings, a mere five daily through services remaining by mid 1939. Through coach working ceased altogether in 1940, after which all services on the branch became pull-and-push connections with London-Hastings semi-fasts at Crowhurst. Bexhill West thus totally lost its 'main line' aura, its business shrinking to a few hundred long-distance commuters, some of whom used it because they preferred to be delivered to the City rather than the West End, and a sprinkling of passengers through the day to intermediate points such as Tunbridge Wells and Tonbridge.

Seen from a window of the Bexhill West train, a Bexhill–Crowhurst set approaches after leaving Combe Haven viaduct on 30th May 1958. Alan A. Jackson

On the last day, 14th June 1964, the 11.05 from Crowhurst calls at a deserted Sidley. Normally the leading 2H Diesel/Electric unit would have sufficed, but presumably in view of anticipated extra traffic a 4S unit has been attached. S.C. Nash

In Southern days various proposals were developed and aborted to form a physical connection with the ex-LB&SCR coastal line, which was just over the road from Bexhill West's forecourt. Sir Herbert Walker put forward a scheme in 1937 for electrification of the Hastings via Tunbridge Wells line, including the Bexhill West branch, which would have been given through London services, the multiple units coupling and uncoupling at Crowhurst. For reasons not apparent in the surviving records, the board refused the plans and also a modified proposal put to it later that year. It is amusing to speculate whether this electrification, which was to have special stock to fit the main line's restricted loading gauge, and which if approved would have been ready before the war began, might have saved the Bexhill West branch from closure in the 1960s.

There was a brief final period of main line glory in 1949-50 when Bopeep tunnel had to be closed for reconstruction. On Sunday 20th November 1949 and from 27th November 1949 until 4th June 1950 inclusive all London-Hastings via Tonbridge trains were temporarily diverted to terminate at Bexhill West. Despite the ample facilities there, the pressure on siding space was such that one train had to be berthed overnight at Sidley. It should perhaps be noted that the 'Schools' Class 4-4-0s used on the London services at this time were always permitted to work over the branch, although required to run at reduced speed.

In SR and early BR days the branch trains were usually ex LB&SCR Billinton 'D3' 0-4-4-T and two car push-pull sets but latterly ex SE&CR 'H' class 0-4-4T were employed. In June 1958 steam working was replaced by two-car diesel-electric units connecting at Crowhurst with the new diesel-electric services between Hastings, Tunbridge Wells and London, giving the branch about 22 return workings daily. Steam operation did not cease on the often-quoted date owing to late delivery of the new units and was also resumed temporarily in March 1959 owing to a shortage of diesel stock. In the 1950s an unadvertised school train operated in term time between Etchingham and Bexhill West. A pull-and-push unit was provided and in later years a diesel-electric set.

The Marples-Beeching purge of BR services brought an end to the branch. Before this, the Sunday services had ceased between 3rd January and 10th April 1960, a portent of things to come. They were never resumed again in the winter period. Under the somewhat questionable assessments used for the exercise, the Bexhill West branch earned a place in the very first swathe of Beeching cuts. Freight services to the two yards were abandoned in September 1963, the date also originally set for passenger closure but the service continued to run until close of traffic on 14th June 1964 to allow the TUCC to hear objections and additional bus services to be arranged between Sidley and Bexhill Central stations. At this time there were some 200 season ticket holders from Bexhill West to London and another 40 or so from Sidley. These formed the main opposition and an attempt was made to appease them by promising better connections at St Leonards for Bexhill Central. At the TUCC hearing, evidence was given that news of the impending closure had stimulated a marked rise in houses put up for sale in the western part of Bexhill and depreciation in house values was likely to follow.

Track was lifted from the branch in 1965 (including the bay and fast roads at Crowhurst) and the local authority purchased much of the railway land. The difficult task of removing the viaduct was postponed until May 1969, when it was dramatically blown up under the eyes of the national media. Ironically, it now seems that the ever-active planners of new roads have their eyes on part of the Bexhill West branch, and if they get their way, a new viaduct will be required at Combe Haven.

Surviving relics of the branch include the goods shed at Sidley, which the Southern had sold to Pepper & Sons, builders' merchants and lime manufacturers, as surplus to rail requirements as long ago as 1929; it is now a store and offices for a coal merchant. The site of the former Sidley freight and passenger stations is a road transport park and council yard. At Bexhill West, the handsome main terminal building can still be admired in its new guise as auction galleries. The remainder of the land here now forms a council-owned industrial estate. Crowhurst station remains open as a commuter railhead, with minimal facilities, having lost its SER platform buildings.

It is salutary to reflect that at a point when we seem about to receive the dubious blessings and benefits of a convoluted scheme for private ownership of rail services, relics at and near Bexhill remind us of the transience and over-optimism of a substantial rail investment by competitive private enterprise some 90 years ago.

The Hants and Sussex DEMUs

Nigel Barnes-Evans and L.A. Mack

Operating in an area more widely known for electric traction, over three decades the diesel-electric multiple units have played as important a role as any other classes of Southern rolling stock. Nigel Barnes-Evans and L.A. Mack trace the history of the Hants and Sussex units.

Above **Unit 1104 stands at Woking soon after going into service and displaying the orange V van end marking. The open guard's door suggests a recent shunt**

At the start of the 1950s, the Bowles Report had suggested that the Southern should produce a fleet of diesel-electric units to operate various services. The thinking behind this document was based on the Region's vast experience with electric unit traction motors. At the time, there were several secondary lines which were drawing unwanted attention to themselves owing to poor returns, and a revitalisation was called for. Whilst other regions opted for diesel-mechanical transmission, this report laid the foundations of the Region's stance of refusing to adopt underfloor powered diesel units.

The SR had resisted underfloor diesel power, not because of what it was but because of what it could not do. The SR requirement was for a diesel train which could operate between fast EMU and express steam services to virtually the same point-to-point standards; the leisurely trundle of overgrown buses which characterised the typical diesel-mechanical designs would have been an operating obstruction. The Southern Railway had had plans to electrify the London–Hastings route in the 1930s, but the need for narrow-bodied (8ft 0ins) stock, which the CM&EE was not prepared to agree to, delayed the scheme until 1939, when it was shelved because of the Second World War.

A small fleet of (possibly 42) 8ft-wide loco-hauled coaches, to be on 57ft underframes (the BR short-wheelbase variety used for

routes with restricted clearances) appears to have been authorised by BR in 1954 for construction in 1956. The sudden availability of funds in the Modernisation Plan allowed the Hastings line to be dieselised.

This was announced late in 1955 before any work had been done on the steam coaches, except for some drawings at Derby design office. It was at one time thought that four 'blank' BR lot numbers, 30181-84 of 1954, represented these, but more recent information indicates those lot numbers as being for a batch of EMUs for the LMR, cancelled in October 1954. There are thus no blank lot numbers for the hypothetical Hastings steam stock.

The Southern found what was basically a marine diesel power unit, redesigned the standard underframe and suspension to take the weight, and because the project was urgent, a batch of seven 6-car units went straight into production. Drawing office time was saved by using Derby's drawings for the trailer coaches. All the coaches had to be designed from scratch because, unlike any other BR passenger-carrying design, they were flat-sided.

The first motor underframes, with their distinctive trapezoidal fan mounting (a steel frame shaped like a pyramid with the top chopped off) were rolled out of Ashford shops about March 1956. By the summer, a diesel engine had been lowered onto a frame in

Eastleigh C&W works. The CM&EE looked at the downward deflection of the under-frame under the load, gave his approval, and body production commenced. The first Hastings unit, 1001, to BR lot numbers 30329-31, late add-ons to the 1956 programme, carried works date 17.1.57; 1007 was dated 13.4.57. There was a short pause and then an extra three units were built (dated 5.57). These were on full-length (ie 64ft) under-frames – not part of the seven-unit approval, but more late add-ons to the 1956 programme as lots 30395-97; they were built out of sequence in the programme because they were needed urgently.

A desperate need to do something about worn-out LSWR carriages and locos in Hampshire led to the first batch of Hampshires (Lot Nos. 30332-33, another add-on to the year's programme). They had the same traction system and similar suspension and auxiliaries to the Hastings, but there the comparison ended; they were to SR restriction 4, BR restriction C1, with 9ft body width and bodies assembled, so far as practicable, on jigs previously used for 2-EPB EMUs. They had a motor brake second open and a driving trailer lavatory composite, but were not gangwayed. The first one, 1101, was shown to the public in August 1957 at Eastleigh Works open day. Most units were given running-in mileage between Fullerton Junction and Andover. The same power unit/generator/traction motor combination was used as in the Hastings units, these being an English Electric 500hp 4-SRKT, coupled to an English Electric generator which fed a pair of English Electric EE507 250hp traction motors.

This batch, numbered 1101-1118, was allocated to Eastleigh. The first workings were between Portsmouth and Southsea and Salisbury (via Southampton Central) and between Southampton and Winchester City over the 'Mid Hants' line. By November, the vehicles were also operating Southampton Terminus–Alton, and Portsmouth and Southsea–Andover Junction (via Botley). By that time the average daily mileage per set was 365.

The effects of these new units on traffic levels was excellent from the start. Staff morale was boosted as drivers leapt at the DEMU training courses. They provided the first regular mainline diesel work in the area. A special staff room was built on the down platform at Eastleigh for the sole use of the drivers, and those working the diesel duties took on the mantle of a new elite! In Hampshire, journey times were cut and passenger levels rocketed. On average, journey times shrunk by 25 per cent, frequencies were improved due to quicker turn round times at the end of runs, and reliability was up also. Loadings rose by 29 per cent in the first six months.

More efficient use of stock resulted, with fuelling available at both Eastleigh and Fratton. Outstabling at Salisbury and Fratton complemented the new purpose-built building for the units at Eastleigh. Engines needed a full overhaul every 450,000 miles, and to facilitate the movement of power units between the various depots and the main works at Eastleigh, a fleet of four special wagons was built. In effect a four-wheel flat wagon, each carried a special steel container which took one whole power unit inside.

By 1960, the Hastings route showed a 40% rise in use compared to 1956. In Hampshire, the levels of use demanded that additional centre coaches be provided for the two car units. This was to come about in 1959, when units 1123-1126 were introduced into traffic as the first purpose-built three car sets. The extra cars for the Hampshires were put into traffic between early August and the end of October 1959, and units 1123-26 followed

immediately. The addition of a third coach meant that a power increase was needed. By using 600hp rated engines the problem was solved. The uprated Hants engines (in 1959/60) came from existing Hastings units, and the existing Hastings units received Hampshire engines. The increase in output was achieved by a larger turbo-charger, but pushed the little four cylinder engine to its limit. The weight of the extra car, although coped with on other lines, immediately proved too much for the steep gradients of the Winchester–Alton line. Units for this line therefore reverted to two cars in 1960, with the units being rotated so as to equalise the mileage run. This practice continued until the line closed.

Sets 1119-1122, specifically introduced in 1958 for use on the Ashford–Hastings, Bexhill West and New Romney lines, stayed two car. The others became three-car units, as they received their additional coach, a Trailer Second Open.

The final phase of building was in 1962, when units 1127-1133 completed the fleet. They had a larger brake van of 14ft 5½ins, and had a smaller route code box as since the last batch, a reduced size blind had become standard. Other differences included tapered windscreens and external window frames. All older units retained the large aperture to the end. The use of oil tail lamps on the DEMUs ended in 1960, when two illuminated red blinds became accepted across the region at the same time as the size of the headcode digits was decreased. This final batch became known as 'Berkshire' units, mainly as they were designed to work Portsmouth–Reading through services.

The last DEMUs to be designed were a slightly modified fleet for use in Sussex and Kent. They were numbered 1301-1319 and became known as Oxted units, eventually coded 3-D. They were allocated to St Leonards and remained there until closure in 1986. Production of the Oxted and Berkshire units proceeded together, but completions were delayed by a shortage of engines and by low morale at Eastleigh Works, which had just been told it was about to be closed. Overall width was 8ft 6ins, and the mountings for the engines were slightly different from the 11xx range, which meant these could not be interchanged.

Anti-wheelslip protection was included. The units were formed of a Motor Brake Second Open, a Trailer Composite with lavatory and a Driving Trailer Second Open. The layout of the intermediate trailer was unusual, with a central side corridor section with four first class compartments and a lavatory, and a second class saloon at each end.

An attempt was at last made to improve the bland image of the DEMUs, the Eastleigh drawing office giving these units a more attractive end moulded from steel reinforced glass fibre with rounded edges, receptacles for the jumpers, and orange handrails. They had a revised layout driver's desk. As with all the three-car units, no gangway between the coaches was provided. This meant restricted access to the lavatory on long journeys, such as London to Brighton via Uckfield. Some Oxteds emerged with orange front headstocks and buffer barrels.

The Oxteds (like the Hastings series) were built to a slightly narrower than standard width, being to restriction 1 to allow use between Tunbridge Wells Central and West, as again a tunnel caused problems for normal width stock. By the time these units were completed, the sound sense of building the whole DEMU fleet was becoming apparent. The totally enclosed power units did not suffer exposure to the weather that other regions' mechanical unit bus-style engines did, and the general reliability and economy of the SR units had also been established.

Early problems of rough riding and excessive engine noise had been tackled to a degree, although replacement of the bogies with the B4/B5 variety in later life would have helped. In an attempt to explore the possibility of solving the vibration problems of these engines, unit 1129 was fitted with a Dorman 12 cylinder engine in 1964. This was rated at 725hp, and whilst making for a quiet and rapid ride, suffered mechanical problems and was later removed. That was the only attempt made to re-engine the units, and their characteristics gradually became tolerated in the light of their otherwise excellent performances.

A rather unusual problem which occurred on the Hastings–Ashford route was that of sheep wool getting into the radiators and combining with oil and deposits to form a solid block! Steam cleaning solved that particular drawback.

In sum the non-electrified passenger network of the region had been given a much healthier look financially.

By 1963, the Fawley branch had become 100% DEMU, and the Alton service from Southampton had acquired 2-car units 1121/1122 from East Sussex and Kent to operate it due to steep gradients hampering the three car units. June 1962 saw the start of through Reading to Portsmouth DEMUs, and the arrival of the Oxted units allowed dieselisation of the remaining East Sussex steam operated routes in January 1964. Hampshire units 1114-1118 moved to the Central Division in May 1964 to serve Three Bridges and the Horsham–Brighton routes.

Despite all this, the completion of the last units roughly coincided with the appearance of the Beeching Plan. This listed many of the lines worked by the DEMUs for closure or truncation. Lines which perished included the following, in order of closure:

Line	Date
Crowhurst–Bexhill West	June 1964
Romney–Andover Junction	September 1964
Totton–Fawley	February 1966
Shoreham–Christ's Hospital	March 1966
Three Bridges–East Grinstead– Groombridge	January 1967
Appledore–New Romney	March 1967
Polegate–Hailsham	September 1968
Uckfield–Lewes	February 1969
Wareham–Swanage	January 1972
Winchester–Alton (after much local opposition)	February 1973
Tunbridge Wells Central– Eridge	July 1985

On the plus side, DEMUs operated stopping services from Eastleigh to Weymouth for a while in the mid-1960s, and made a brief appearance on the Lymington branch between April and May 1967, pending electrification. When this was completed to Bournemouth in 1967, the Reading to Portsmouth service was split in two halves, with DEMUs working Basingstoke to Reading and also Eastleigh to Portsmouth. Electric units covered the main line stretches remaining as part of the new traffic patterns. The through workings recommenced in 1981! The removal of the Uckfield to Lewes link meant that considerable dead mileage had to be incurred to enable the 3-Ds, then based at St Leonards near Hastings, to return there for fuelling.

Plans for an underfloor engined DEMU for use on the Cardiff–Portsmouth–Brighton route were examined in the mid-1960s, based on earlier schemes by BR at Derby using converted hauled coaching stock. The project actually got to the stage of producing a specification for cross country use. The extra power required was to come from a robust English Electric power unit of 900hp. It all came to nothing in the end, which condemned that route to several more years in the wilderness with inappropriate stock, including 3-Hs for a while.

A short-lived 4-coach unit existed in September/October 1964, with motor and trailer from 1107, trailer from 1129 and motor from 1126. This was due to the fact that 1107's Driving Trailer was 'helping Police with their enquiries' after a murder occurred in it, and it was needed for forensic analysis.

Mention should be made of a few points of detail at this stage. All DEMUs started service in all-over plain dark green livery, with black coach ends and underframes. Lettering was in an old-gold colour. Upholstery trim in the second class was in red-based patterns, variously rep or moquette, except in the Oxteds, which were trimmed in the Kent Coast electric 'Trojan' rep. First class trim was in varieties of green rep except in 1101-1118, which had a blue and grey moquette. On the first major overhaul, 'Trojan' was used for all second class accommodation. All early units had tall angular numerals in the headcode boxes, and air whistles were fitted as standard. By 1964 small yellow warning panels had appeared on all units, with horns replacing the whistles. 3-H units had carried orange 'V's at the brake van ends from 1960 onwards, to show platform staff which end to deal with the parcels and luggage. On the subject of luggage space, units 1101-1118 and 1120-1126 all had the second class compartment between the driving cab and first class accommodation converted into extra van space in 1963. In some cases, this reverted to passenger use as a first class compartment on some units in later days, particularly those working on the Oxted line.

When the small yellow panels were applied from 1964, a black inverted solid triangle was painted over the yellow. The new Corporate Image was introduced in 1965, and the following year the DEMUs started to emerge from overhaul in all-over plain blue livery with initially the small yellow warning panels, which gave way to full yellow ends from 1967. The new BR logo replaced the lion and wheel emblem at that time. Being main line stock the Hastings units soon went into blue and grey livery, and few went through the plain blue stage. All units carried white lettering and had the smaller route code numerals by this time.

Units except the 3-Ds had small cast plates giving the main dimensions of each unit attached to the cab ends. The Oxteds had these details painted on instead. All DEMUs had buck-eye couplings throughout, with automatic air and electro-pneumatic brakes. 300 gallon fuel tanks on the power cars gave a range of about 750 miles on a full tank. It is a mark of the DEMUs' safety record that the accident at Hither Green in November 1967 when two Hastings units derailed at high speed was the only real act of destruction that they have suffered in their long lives to date.

The 1970s saw all the SR DEMUs going about their business in their usual reliable fashion. Major overhaul took place at Eastleigh, with work of a lesser nature being undertaken at St Leonards, Chart Leacon or Selhurst. This often included quite demanding tasks such as engine changes. All three-car units were in the all-over blue livery, which only really looked good when freshly applied.

A route of considerable length which would have benefited from the use of the six-car Hastings units now wandering widely, that from Portsmouth to Bristol, was booked to be worked by the 3-Hs from May 1973 to May 1977. While working this service, the doors of the power car and centre trailer had yellow stickers to warn passengers that there was no access to a lavatory in these vehicles.

It is a measure of how low a regard the service received that quite unsuitable 3-Hs had a four year reign. They were to return to duty on this vital cross-country route much later, but in a more limited way. Long distance duty again proved their usefulness, but also exposed their now dated design. A spin-off which resulted from the training of Bristol drivers on DEMU stock was that more excursion work to this part of the country resulted for the Hastings units. 1973 saw BR go computerised in much of its operating facilities, and the DEMUs acquired a new three-digit classification. The Hastings sets became classes 201-203, the Hampshires 205, and the Oxteds 207. At this stage, the actual unit numbers were not altered.

A Sunday parade of DEMUs at Tunbridge Wells West. Oxted 3Ds present in this July 1985 view include 1307/1303/1304. S. Blackman

At Portcreek Junction near Hilsea, 205 unit 1131 is seen on an Eastleigh–Portsmouth service in June 1982. Brian Morrison

Below **Units pose at Eastleigh in 1986 in process of being exchanged on a Reading–Portsmouth working. The smaller van space on 3D (Oxted) 207013 on the left is still a problem compared with the commodious accommodation on the Hampshire 3H No.205027. The Oxted units had been transferred after service reductions on the Central Division.** N. Barnes-Evans

1979 also saw the remaining four two-coach 3-Hs, Nos.1119-1122, made up to three coaches, but again operating needs overrode other considerations. The four 'new' vehicles required were actually ex 2EPB electric unit driving trailers which had been adapted in 1965 to run with Hastings line coaches to form six 3-R diesel units for use on the Reading–Tonbridge line. When most of the 3-R units were disbanded in 1979 these driving trailers were available for further use. Nos. 1121 and 1122 each received one of these vehicles as a centre trailer, as did 1103 and 1104 whose original trailer seconds went into 1119 and 1120 instead, to bring them belatedly into the 3-H fold. To further confuse the issue, the unit numbered 1121 at the time was an identity change with 1108 this had happened in 1974 when the original 1121 took the centre coach of 1108. The units with the former 3-R driving trailers at the centre were classified 3-T ('trailer') and renumbered 1401-1404. The control equipment in the unused driving cabs was isolated, but no attempt was made to reinstate the seating in the luggage area and so they had fewer seats than a standard 3-H.

The impending life-expiry of some of the DEMUs, in particular the Hastings units, meant that replacement stock had to be found. It was decided to electrify the Hastings line and the London services went over to EMUs in May 1986. Nearly all the narrow bodied stock was retired.

The electrification of the East Grinstead line in October 1987 led to the first planned withdrawals of Oxted units. Both 3-H and 3-D suffered reductions in their numbers. Twelve of the 19 Oxteds perished, as did a batch of 205s.

The first and only example of a full updating of these clases occurred back in 1979 when 1111, later 205101, was totally gutted and rebuilt at Eastleigh Works. In its new form, it had second class accommodation only, had fluorescent lighting fitted throughout and had gangways created between the coaches, but not at the unit ends. Public address was added, and asbestos was removed from the whole unit. The driver's desk was replaced with a 4-VEP (423) style one with four-position controller, and all the seating changed to VEP type also, with plastic-coated headrests and making use of seat ends from withdrawn SUB coaches. The vivid yellow interior finish with false ceilings may not have been too restful on the eyes but, for a few thousand pounds, it gave an indication of what could be achieved. The control system was modified to enable it to run in multiple with 'EP' braked EMU stock, although this was never tried.

This Page Upper **Hampshire DEMU 1101 crosses the Broom Channel on a Portsmouth Harbour to Salisbury trip in 1982.** Brian Morrison

This Page Lower **The wide route availability of the DEMUs allowed them to perform odd duties. No.205033 and another unit stand in the unlikely setting of the MOD complex at Bramley, Hants on 1st March 1987. They worked a special on the occasion of the closure of the internal rail network.** A. French

Facing Page Upper **Due to major weekend engineering works at Sevenoaks in May 1993, trains from Tonbridge to Charing Cross were diverted via Redhill and provided the unusual sight of DEMUs working into Charing Cross. Having worked the 11.15 Tonbridge to Charing Cross additional on 15th May 1993, Nos.205008/016 approach Waterloo East with the return working.** Brian Morrison

Facing Page Lower **A 'Kenny Belle' service from Clapham Junction arrives at Kensington Olympia on 23rd July 1993, the last day of the 207s operating this service prior to EMUs taking over.** Brian Morrison

The prototype 'New Generation' DEMUs which followed three years later, the class 210, came out at about £450,000 each. It was a solid design, but as it came to nothing, mainly on cost grounds, one can't help but feel that most of that cash could have provided the long-suffering travellers in the 205s and 207s with a more modern environment in the years since then. A number of Mark II bodied DEMUs were built for Northern Ireland Railways. They featured the same power unit as the English ones, but were naturally a step up in terms of passenger environment. Later a 210 type of body, actually a diesel powered class 455 EMU, again went to Ireland, whilst our 1957 type examples rumbled on.

In May 1990, the lines from Portsmouth to Southampton were given the third rail treatment, with any surplus units going to Selhurst to increase their pool for use on the Uckfield line. This marked the end of the long through workings between Reading and Portsmouth via Eastleigh. The next summer saw an end to the use of DEMUs between Southampton and Salisbury, the odd diagrammed Bristol service going at that time also. These had recommenced back in May 1990.

The native 207s which had virtually disappeared from their stamping grounds, reappeared in the form of partly refurbished two coach units, the 207/1s, in 1991. They provide a dedicated fleet of sets for the Hastings–Ashford 'Marsh Link' service. The three units were formed by removing the centre trailer of three 207s, fitting a gangway between the two remaning coaches, and generally freshening them up with fluorescent lighting in the saloons. This work was carried out at Selhurst and Eastleigh. The 2-car 207/1 units have no toilets for quite a long journey.

Eastleigh units, which included the last four three coach 3-Ds, carried on their daily outings between Salisbury, Basingstoke and Reading until May 1993, also covering the Monday-Friday peak hour Clapham Junction to Kensington Olympia duties. This service had always been an inconvenient one to provide stock for as it was not electrified until 1993. The future for the remaining examples of the 205s and 207s appears mixed. The change to New Generation diesel units on the routes covered by the Eastleigh based examples took place in May 1993. The Clapham Junction–Kensington service received EMUs from 26th July 1993, its electrification having been carried out in connection with its future use by Channel Tunnel trains. Thus an end has come to an association which has lasted 36 years. Hampshire units, built in that county, and serving it consistently well for all those years, finally left the area.

All remaining units are now concentrated on Selhurst. A large scale reformation exercise will see ten three-coach units formed out of the best vehicles available. These should see out their days on the Uckfield route. The self-contained Marsh Link will give the three 207/1s use for a while yet, and the sole improved 205101, now reduced to two coaches, will be spare for use as and when needed.

Rather like the way that steam performed on the Southern right up to the virtual end of that form of traction on BR, it seems that diesel units will continue a while yet in this third-rail network.

The address of the Hampshire & Sussex Units Preservation Society is 58 Wavell Way, Stanmore, Winchester, Hants, SO22 4EG. For details please send an sae.

Valuable help was provided with this article by Lawrie Bowles and David Brown.

Pullman Car Specials

J.J. Smith

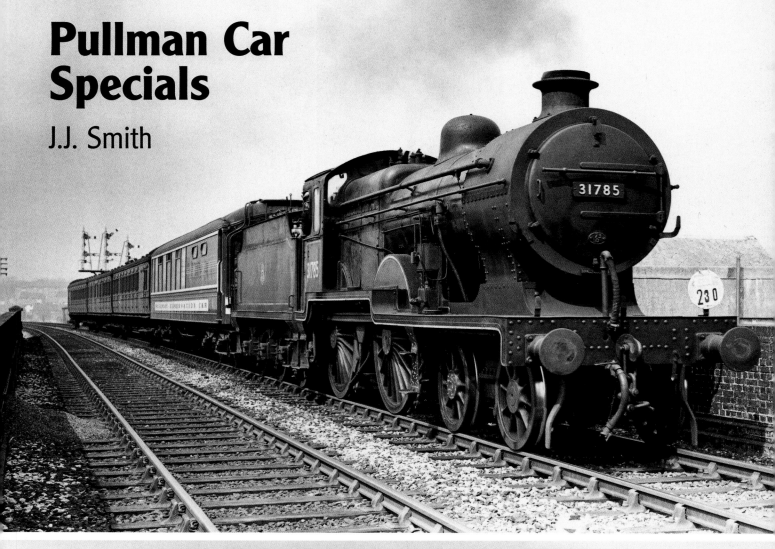

Above **Sunday 29th April 1956 saw Pullman Observation Car No.13 leave Victoria on a morning service for Tunbridge Wells West, where it was attached to the 1.00pm Sevenoaks–Brighton seen here at Lewes. L1 Class 31785 has reduced speed for the sinuous approach over bridge and viaduct leading to a 1 in 50 descent over the junction into Lewes station. Little remains of this scene today. The three vehicles behind the car form one of the numerous ex-SECR 'Rover' sets which were for so long a familiar feature of the Central and Eastern sections of the SR. Car No.13 was one of several vehicles which started life in 1918 as LNWR ambulance coaches and were reconstructed as conventional Pullmans in 1921. Together with a car of similar ancestry, No.14, it was converted to the form seen here in 1947 for use in the *Devon Belle* between Waterloo and Ilfracombe. After cessation of that service in 1955 both cars were sold to BR, who used them on scenic lines in Wales and Scotland.**

For many years after the second world war the Royal Train from Victoria to Tattenham Corner on Derby Day was formed of Pullman cars as seen here near Woodmansterne on 6th June 1953. Stewarts Lane cleaners always did a good job with the locomotive, as is evident from the sparkling condition of 'Schools' Class No.30915 *Brighton*.

Above **A view in March 1958 shows more modern motive power in the shape of Ivatt class 2 2-6-2T 41291 of Stewarts Lane depot on a 6-car rake destined for service on the Eastern region.**

Until 1960 the stock for the Bournemouth Belle was kept at Stewarts Lane, conveniently situated for loading stores from the 'Battersea Commissary Depot' as the Pullman Car Company's nearby depot was officially known. The 01 class 31370 seen here at Longbridge Junction has taken over from an M7 0-4-4 at Clapham Junction and is returning the cars to their nocturnal abode. The date is 10th June 1959, four days before the conductor rail on the Ludgate lines (the farther pair in the picture) was energised. A series of rationalisations since 1959 has resulted in a much simplified layout at Longhedge. It is only recently in connection with the Channel Tunnel scheme that third rail electrification has been extended to the West London Extension line.

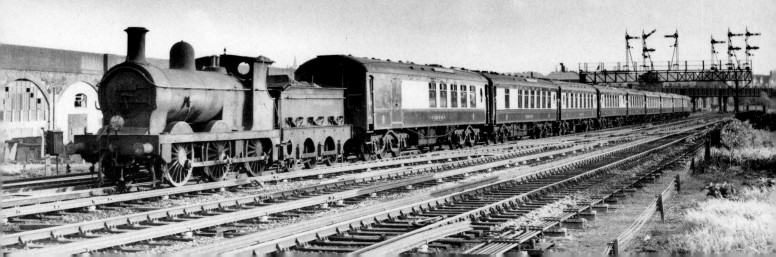

Above **In general, all maintenance of cars above underframe level was dealt with at Preston Park, where the company's works had been relocated from Longhedge (Battersea) in 1928. Work on the frames and running gear was carried out at the BR works at Lancing in the case of cars allocated to the Southern and Western regions, Doncaster in the case of those working out of King's Cross, and at BR's Selhurst repair depot in the case of the Brighton Belle units. Cars going into Lancing works, if not forming part of a special train, usually arrived on the daily freight train from Brighton Top yard, a rare dispensation from the rule that coaching stock, especially catering vehicles with their fragile contents, should not be moved by goods services. Cars outshopped from Lancing were 'run in' on the 11.33am 'stock train'. This usually comprised a miscellany of coaching stock and its running was arranged as soon as sufficient vehicles had accumulated. Typically it ran to one of the London carriage depots, dropping off vehicles for other destinations en route. Cars destined for Preston Park shops were detached at Redhill and sent back down the line on the Brighton/Eastbourne/Hastings portion of the 7.35am Birkenhead–Ramsgate/Margate inter-regional train, as seen here leaving Redhill at 2.45pm with car *Octavia* on 1st March 1955. As reversal was involved at Brighton, the car could be shunted direct to the shops as soon as the train had left for Eastbourne and (after another reversal) Hastings. Shortly after the date of this photograph it was decreed that cars ex Lancing works should be 'run in' at least as far as East Croydon, so bringing an end to the practice depicted. Tonbridge D class No.31737 commenced its work with the 6.09am Sevenoaks–Brighton, working up to Redhill on the corresponding northbound portion of the Birkenhead train (9.25am ex Hastings), which on this date will have been composed of Western Region coaches, the stock alternating daily.**

Facing Page Upper **Drummond T9 Class 30718 was a rare visitor to Horsted Keynes on 25th May 1955 hauling the 5.18pm ex Brighton with Pullman car *Savona* bringing up the rear. The track layout at Horsted Keynes was peculiar. The line, served by two platform faces, furthest from the camera, was always used as a down line, but originally was available only for trains to the Sheffield Park line, the junction with the Ardingly line being in the foreground. Later the divergence of the two routes in the down direction was moved to the far end of the station and the line seen to the left of the unsheltered island platform, previously used by down trains to Ardingly, became the up line from Ardingly, the former up line becoming a siding.**

Facing Page Lower **On 24th September 1955 recently renovated Parlour Brake car No.80 is seen at Canonbury on a special working from East Croydon. Norwood Class C2X No.32547 is about to leave for Dalston Junction to turn on the triangle before making for home. N2 Class No.69547 has taken over for the final short journey to Finsbury Park.**

Above **The 1.50pm train from Blackwall pauses at Leman Street station, one stop away from Fenchurch Street, in March 1925.** Ken Nunn

From Cable Haulage to Computer Control

H.P. White

London's newest line, Docklands Light Rail, uses much of the right-of-way and infrastructure of one of London's oldest, the Blackwall. The author traces the complex history of the railways in the area now served by the DLR.

In the early years of the nineteenth century, London — and particularly its port — was spreading downstream along the north bank of the Thames out towards Blackwall. The West India Docks were opened in 1802 and the East India in 1806. In 1810 they were connected to the City by the East India Dock Road. Houses and industry spread along this, but to the south stretched an undeveloped Isle of Dogs and to the north common land and fields separated Poplar from Bow.

Steamers were increasing passenger traffic on the River. Services included the 'short ferry' to Greenwich and the 'long' to Gravesend; to Margate and Ramsgate; and across the Channel to Holland. In the 1830s the 'long ferry' alone was carrying some million passengers annually. Most of these steamers called at Brunswick Wharf, Blackwall. To speed communication between the City and Brunswick Wharf and thus reduce the time spent on the steamers, the Commercial Railway was incorporated on 28th July 1836 to build a line from Minories to Blackwall. In 1839 it became the London & Blackwall Railway. George Stephenson was the Engineer jointly with G.P. Bidder (known as 'The Calculating Boy' from his childhood ability at mental arithmetic).

The line, which was just over 3½ miles long, had several unusual features. Two and a quarter miles were on a brick viaduct, which as we shall see is still in use. It was of 5 foot gauge and was cable operated. The Lord Mayor and a party of dignitaries travelled down it on 4th July 1840 and public service started two days later. A single track was in operation, but a second track came into use on 3rd August allowing a 15-minute service. The original intermediate stations were Limehouse, West India Dock and Poplar, but by the end of the year Shadwell and Stepney, later Stepney East, had been added. Cannon Street Road, between Minories and Shadwell, was opened on 21st August 1842, but closed in 1848.

A 415 yard extension to the more convenient Fenchurch Street opened on 2nd August 1841. The 1846 Royal Commission on London Traffic was told of a 50 per cent increase in traffic as a consequence. In 1844 of the 331,644 passengers landed and embarked at Gravesend, over 200,000 had used the Blackwall railway.

The method of operation was complicated. Each line was operated separately. The train of 4-wheeled carriages, of five tons apiece, was made up of one or more vehicles for the

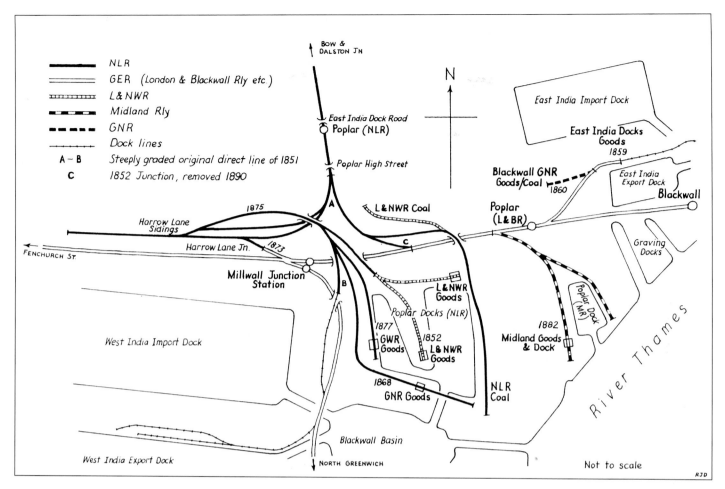

intermediate stations as well as for Blackwall. They were run down to Minories by gravity, where they were attached to the endless rope. On receiving the signal, the Blackwall engine would begin hauling. The coaches for the intermediate stations would be detached by the guards who travelled on each and who would bring it to a halt using a brake, the rest of the train rumbling on non-stop. Meanwhile coaches from the inter-mediate stations would be attached to the rope and arrive at Blackwall ahead of the section from Fenchurch Street. The return would be made in a similar way, the coaches being released by the guards at Minories to run by their own momentum up to the terminus.

The line was not without its problems, which included the cables breaking. One winter, sailors on their way to Blackwall were seen playing snowballs on the track during one breakdown. More seriously there were accidents to workers, culminating in the death of the Minories station master, who was caught up in the rope and crushed to death against the drum.

The future of the steamer traffic was threatened by the opening of the South Eastern's line to Ramsgate and Margate in 1846 and more particularly its North Kent line in 1849 which served the towns on the south bank as far as the Medway. Local traffic was limited, so the Company looked to other sources of revenue, particularly through ending its isolation. Accordingly it was regauged to standard and converted to locomotive haulage, the last rope hauled train running on 14th February 1849. This was in connection with the opening on 2nd April 1849 of a link from Stepney to the Eastern Counties line at Bow Junction (GE), a mile west of Stratford station. But such was the intransigence of the ECR the junction was not used at first, and through workings began in 1854.

Of more immediate success was the junction with the North London. The East & West India Docks & Birmingham Junction Company was established in 1846 for a line from Primrose Hill to the docks. In 1853 this became the North London Railway. The link from the latter's Bow Road station to Bow Junction (NLR), on the Stratford link, was opened on 26th September 1850 and Fenchurch Street became the city terminus of the North London, a 15-minute service to Islington being inaugurated. In 1854 the London, Tilbury & Southend trains arrived via Forest Gate and Stratford. But on 31st March 1858 their direct line from Barking was opened to Bow Junction (LTS), later Gas Factory Junction, 10 chains north of the NLR junction. The London & Blackwall was now deriving considerable rental for use of Fenchurch street and its approaches.

On 1st November 1865 the North London opened its more conveniently approached Broad Street station. A 15-minute service began between Broad Street and Fenchurch Street, but was diverted to Poplar (NLR) on 1st August 1866.

The Great Eastern was incorporated in 1862, taking over the Eastern Counties. From 1st January 1866 the London & Blackwall was leased to the GER for 999 years, the GER guaranteeing 4½ per cent on its capital stock. The GER worked the line, but the Company remained independent until 1923, when it was absorbed into the LNER.

The Blackwall was also interested in developing goods traffic to the Docks, as was the North London, for that was originally to be a principal function of the latter.

Cable hauled composite coach, London & Blackwall Railway. The apparatus worked by a guard for connecting with the endless rope can be seen at the right hand end.

Accordingly it was opened to Poplar Docks, with a connection to the Blackwall Railway, in 1851/1852. The layout was complex and a detailed account is outside the scope of this article. Suffice to say that in the 1870s Harrow Lane Yard was laid out by the North London on the north side of the Blackwall and reached from their line at Poplar High Street Junction (just south of Poplar passenger station). Here a reversal was needed to a fan of connections to the docks passing over the Blackwall.

Most railway companies sought access to the Thames. This was not necessarily at or near the principal dock systems. Much of the import and export cargoes were transferred to and from the ships by lighter and it was access to lighter wharves which was the object. In the end, in the Poplar area there were depots owned not only by the Blackwall and North London, but by the LNWR, Midland, Great Northern and Great Western.

On 1st September 1870 the North London inaugurated a service to Blackwall over the reconstructed 1852 curve. But the passenger traffic was in decline and from 1st July 1890 Poplar (NLR) again became the terminus for Broad Street trains. The connecting spur was removed and the only connection with the Blackwall line was via Poplar High Street Junction and Harrow Lane. The layout in the area was completed when the Blackwall opened a north to east spur for freight in April 1880 at Stepney from Salmon's Lane Junction, on the Stratford link, to Limehouse Junction. It should also be recorded that the Blackwall encouraged other lines to establish goods depots on the section between Fenchurch Street and Shadwell. Eventually there were five in addition to the Blackwall's at Goodmans Yard (Minories).

Meanwhile the dock traffic was increasing. The West India Docks were enlarged in the 1840s and Millwall Dock was added in 1868. Housing for dock workers was laid out in Millwall and Cubitt Town, which dates from 1843, while dock-related industries grew up around the docks and along the river bank.

To serve this area a railway system was laid out, the 'trunk' being a 1.5 mile line from the Blackwall at Millwall Junction, where a station was provided. It was authorised under the title of the Millwall Extension Railway by the Blackwall's Act of 19th June 1865. But its ownership was complicated. The Blackwall owned 5 chains at the north end and 31 chains at the south. Between, the London & India Docks Company owned 41 chains and the Millwall Dock Company 52 chains. Both these lengths eventually passed to the Port of London Authority on its formation in 1909.

The line was opened to Millwall Dock on 18th December 1871, when a passenger service was inaugurated. This was extended over the still-existing viaduct to North Greenwich (Cubitt Town) on the bank of the River on 29th July 1872. Beside the local traffic there was that in connection with the ferry thence to Greenwich. This was bought by the Blackwall and GER. As late as 1900 this carried 1.3 million passengers, but with the opening by the LCC of the present foot tunnel in 1902, the ferry ceased operations.

Passenger services on the Millwall Extension were somewhat bizarre and there was never through running beyond Millwall Junction. Because of the fire risk to warehouses and sailing ships, many of them wood-built, horses were used until the insurance companies permitted steam traction in 1880.

The interior of Blackwall station after closure, much less impressive than the exterior, and rather cramped for a frequent service. Brunswick Wharf is on the right and the East India Dock to the left.
H.J. Patterson Rutherford

But weight restrictions meant that three diminutive tank locomotives were employed hauling small four-wheeled coaches.

The frequent service over the Blackwall continued for the remainder of the century. Though the steamer traffic from Brunswick wharf continued to decline, it remained a destination for days out for East Enders, while the line was well used by dockers, sailors and other workers connected with port activities.

In 1906 there were 50 departures (Mons-Fris) from Fenchurch Street to Blackwall, though not at regular intervals. The journey time was 16 minutes. From Millwall Junction there were 59 departures on the Extension, the 1½ mile journey taking 10 minutes, including two intermediate stops at South Dock and Millwall Dock. An interesting feature of the Extension was the ten extra services on Saturday evenings, with no connections at Millwall Junction.

By 1920 there had been certain changes in the level of service. There were now 57 departures for Blackwall, but only 31 from Millwall Junction, while the Saturday extras had disappeared. The frequency of the service however hid the decline in patronage. Phones had replaced the need for messengers to communicate between the shipping offices around Fenchurch Street and the ships and wharves, while electric trams had reduced local traffic between Poplar and the City. The LNER were considering closure when the General Strike of 1926 brought matters to a head. Trains ceased to run from 4th May, never to be resumed. Freight traffic continued, but the section from Glengall Road to North Greenwich never had any and the track was removed. Fortunately the viaduct was left largely intact. The impressive Blackwall station building, a large two storey Italianate structure, designed by William Tite, architect of Nine Elms and Southampton Terminus, lasted for many years, being finally demolished to make way for the power station of 1954. It fronted a small station with three platform faces.

The impressive frontage of Blackwall station, designed by Sir William Tite, after closure in 1926. It was demolished in the late 1940s to make way for a power station. Brunswick Wharf is in the background.
Railway Magazine

On the Stratford line the GE services as well as the LTS remained at a high level. In 1920 there were 68 departures (Mons-Fris) from Fenchurch to Stratford and beyond to a wide variety of destinations on the Epping line, the Fairlop Loop and the North Woolwich line and its branches. As for the North London service from Poplar, the only reduction by 1920 was that the off-peak service was now half-hourly.

Freight traffic was of course important and remained so after withdrawal of passenger services east of Stepney. In 1920 there were nine departures (Mons-Fris) from Millwall Junction; three were conditional, while one was for Goodman's Yard, the others using the Limehouse–Salmon's Lane curve. The NLR timetable shows 19 departures from Poplar and several more from Devons Road. There were also two parcels trains, one of which included milk empties. There were trains serving the inner goods depots on the approach to Fenchurch Street.

Top **The end of the Millwall Junction Railway at North Greenwich with the River Thames in the background.**
E. Pouteau/Alan A. Jackson collection.

Above Left **North Greenwich station, Millwall Junction Railway, c.1901.** Alan A. Jackson collection.

Above Right **The Millwall Extension train at a location thought to be South Dock. The tiny 2-4-0 tank locos and elderly four-wheeled coaches maintained the service to the end because of weight restrictions.**
D. Taylor collection

Left **The down platform at Limehouse in July 1921 looking towards Stepney East (now Limehouse). Note the low wooden platform. No money had been spent in improving the stations. Note Limehouse Church in the background; the site is about midway between Limehouse and Westferry DLR stations.**
D. Taylor collection

The 1939-45 war saw the final decline to extinction of the inner London suburban services. That between Poplar and Broad Street ceased on 15th May 1944 as a result of bomb damage. Ticket offices remained open for the sale of workmen's tickets valid on replacement bus services until 23rd April 1945, but the trains were permanently withdrawn. Meanwhile Leman Street and Shadwell had closed on 7th July 1941. On the Stratford extension Burdett Road closed on 21st April 1941. Bow Road, the other intermediate station, had a chequered career. Closed at the same time, the LNER re-opened it twice before final closure from 7th November 1949. On that date all the former GE services from Fenchurch Street ceased, leaving the terminus in the sole possession of LTS trains and Stepney East as the only open station remaining on the Blackwall's lines, other than Fenchurch Street.

The Stratford line was electrified from the same day as part of the Liverpool Street scheme. A shuttle service was proposed from Stratford, where a bay platform was provided in the new suburban station. But this never materialised, the line's sole use being for interchange of stock after the LTS electrification on 1962.

The docks traffic continued at a high level until the early 1950s, but thereafter, as more and more was diverted to road, it began to fall, at an accelerated speed after 1960 with the decline of the inner docks. The lines became ever more run down and eventually closure took place, though not before a new connection had been built across the route of the Blackwall Railway from Poplar (NLR) to Poplar Docks in 1968, replacing the connection via Harrow Lane sidings. Access to Millwall docks had been severed in 1967 and to Poplar Dock by 1974. The Limehouse–Salmon's Lane curve closed in 1962 and by 1967 all the inner goods stations west of Shadwell had closed. Scrap metal traffic via the new connection at Poplar and what was latterly a single track from Victoria Park, continued until October 1981.

Containerisation of general cargo meant that one dock berth could now handle as much cargo as eight to ten traditional ones. The PLA concentrated the whole of its operations on an enlarged Tilbury and by 1981 closed not only the East and West India and Millwall Docks, but the Royal Docks as well. The Isle of Dogs, an area almost half as large again as the City, was becoming an area of dereliction, for the riverside wharves and the port based industries were in decline.

Top **A railtour train joins the North London line at High Street Junction. The DMU is almost precisely on the line of the Docklands Light Railway from Poplar station.** H.P. White

Centre **The special train passes the remains of South Bromley station (North London Rly). The location is immediately north of Devons Road station on the DLR.** H.P. White

Right **Poplar L&BR, looking west, in November 1954. The freight branch into the East India Docks curves away in the right foreground.** Alan A. Jackson

Bank signalbox just west of Millwall Junction in May 1956, looking east, with ex-Midland Railway battery loco 1550 (BR BEL 1), left, and ex LMSR 0-6-0T 47484, right. Alan A. Jackson

Millwall Junction Box, looking east to the station, November 1954. Alan A. Jackson

Below Left The remains of North Greenwich station, west side looking south to the Thames, on 15th February 1964. Alan A. Jackson

Below Right North Greenwich station, west side, looking north on the same day. Alan A. Jackson

To deal with the urgent problem, in 1981 the London Docklands Development Corporation (LDDC) was set up. Its area included that of the Royal Docks, where the problems were essentially the same. The new body's powers were very wide-ranging. It was soon realised that economic and social redevelopment depended on development of a transport system adequate for the area's new role, for the existing road system and bus network were both inadequate. At first the Department of Transport took the untenable view that full land use rehabilitation could be possible if based on a bus/car system. It was soon realised a rail system would also be needed to attract developers.

Various proposals for a light rail system were considered and in October 1982 Government approval was secured. After that the lead time was remarkably short. In 1984 the Docklands Light Railway Act authorised the Isle of Dogs section using much of the right of way of the Blackwall and Millwall Extension. At the time the line northward from Poplar was not yet agreed. At first the proposal was to use the right of way of the North London to Bow with street running westward along the A11 to Mile End. But it was finally decided to use the Blackwall's extension from Bow and the 1949 bay platform at Stratford. This was authorised by the 1985 Act.

Without street running, 'state of the art' automation was possible and driverless trains were adopted. Current at 740 volts DC was to be picked up from third rail. Stations were to be unstaffed, with automatic ticket issuing and penalty fares. The trains, a pair of articulated cars, were to be staffed by 'Train Captains' who not only examined tickets and dealt with queries, but in emergency or when the central computer went down, could drive the trains from manual control, though at reduced speed.

Construction went ahead rapidly and resulted in an immediate increase in land values — from an average of £300,000 an acre to £2 million. The 7.5 miles of line with 15 public stations was officially opened by H.M. The Queen on 30th July 1987 and public service was inaugurated, amid some chaos, on 31st August. Though local management was practically autonomous, the system was an integral part of London Regional Transport.

As has been well documented elsewhere, the capacity of the system had to be upgraded almost as soon as it was opened, work starting in 1988. This was a direct consequence of insufficient funding being made available at the initial stage, with the consequent mismatch between planning for land use and for transport. In 1987 it had been calculated that daily user would reach 22,000 per day by 1991. In fact by December 1989 the average rate had reached 33,000 and in July on the occasion of the tall ships race, 44,000 had been conveyed in a single day.

Tower Gateway, on the south side of the quadruple tracked approach to Fenchurch Street station, as has been said, is at almost the precise location of the Blackwall's original Minories station. It has a spacious concourse and a platform with two faces. Like all the other stations, it is unstaffed. The line is on a viaduct alongside BR and the original Blackwall formation. Immediately on the right, the later extension to Bank descends to its tunnel mouth from Leman Street Junction. Some way further, near Cannon Street Road, the BR tracks have been reduced to two and the DLR then runs on the Blackwall viaduct. At Limehouse station (renamed from Stepney East), where the Blackwall's Stratford extension diverged, there are platforms on the BR and DLR lines. The viaduct now skirts the Regent's Canal Dock (Limehouse Basin) and the viaduct of the Limehouse–Salmon's Lane curve can be seen on the left. The Blackwall's viaduct is followed to its end, beyond Westferry station. Ahead looms the Delta junction with its steep grades and sharp curves.

Assuming our train is for Island Gardens, it curves round onto the new viaduct and route over the sheets of water of the West India Docks and through the complex of office blocks and high-tech industry, with the 770 foot Canary Wharf building towering over all. At the immediate southern end of the junction is West India Quay station. This has been rebuilt as two island platforms to accommodate the short length of quadruple track from the Delta to just short of Canary Wharf. At Canary Wharf it is worth alighting to have a look at the magnificent station. Eventually the line bends sharply left and beyond South Quay station sharply right to avoid Millwall Dock and join the old right of way of the Millwall Extension beyond Crossharbour station, which serves the Asda hypermarket and the London Arena, a large entertainment centre.

Beyond Mudchute station (so-called because the area was one where spoil from dredging the river was discharged) the line is single and traverses the 27 arch viaduct over Millwall Park and which saw no trains between 1926 and 1987. It was built to accommodate only a single track. Island Gardens terminus is at the end, a trifle short of the river bank on which North Greenwich station stood, its site occupied by a rowing club. There is an excellent panorama of the Royal Naval College and the other features of Greenwich. The foot tunnel is only yards away from that to the station. A popular tour includes the Tower of London, the DLR, the tunnel, Greenwich and return by river. It is now proposed to extend the DLR to Lewisham, which would mean putting it underground from Crossharbour (with a new station at Island Gardens).

From Canary Wharf, Stratford-bound trains negotiate the junctions and descend to ground level via Poplar station. This is more or less on the site of Millwall Junction, while on the north side is the line's depot and control centre on the site of Harrow Lane Yard. The line curves sharply, as only light rail can, to the left, the Beckton Extension continuing straight on, the eastbound line being taken over the Stratford lines by a flyover.

The line now follows the roadbed of the North London. All Saints station is on the site of the North London one. After passing the site of South Bromley, crossing Limehouse Cut (connecting the River Lea with Limehouse Basin) there is an industrial estate on the right which is on the site of the NLR carriage sheds and loco depot. Beyond, the line passes under the parallel lines of the LTS, the BR trains having diverged from our route at Limehouse, and the District Line to Upminster.

Bow Church station is on the south side of the bridge under Bow Road, the NLR's was on the north side and traces of the old station can be distinguished. Immediately beyond, the line becomes single and climbs by a new curve from the NLR line up to join the main line out of Liverpool Street. To the north, the NLR has been abandoned as far as the site of Victoria Park Junction on the existing line from Dalston Kingsland to Stratford, most of it being occupied by the A102(M).

The lines from Liverpool Street are joined at the former Bow Junction signal box and from here the DLR occupies the former up Fenchurch Street line. The mile section to Stratford is broken by a passing loop at Pudding Mill Lane, where a station is planned at some time in the future. The DLR ends in the single-line bay platform at the end of the up interchange platform between the Central Line trains on the outer face and the Liverpool Street main line ones on the inner.

The Beckton Extension is elevated to the River Lea crossing, passing to the north of the Blackwall's right of way, now completely obscured, and with stations at Blackwall and East India. Beyond the River Lea it can be said to have passed outside the area under review, that served by the Blackwall.

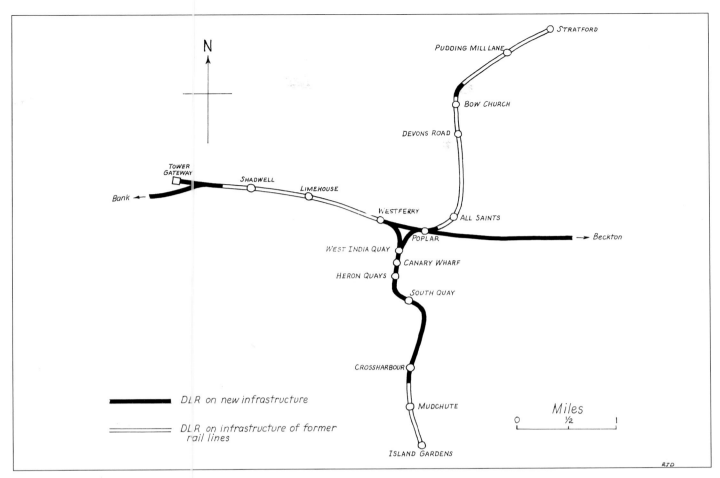

Map showing DLR routes with stations: Stratford, Pudding Mill Lane, Bow Church, Devons Road, All Saints, Tower Gateway, Shadwell, Limehouse, Westferry, Poplar, West India Quay, Canary Wharf, Heron Quays, South Quay, Crossharbour, Mudchute, Island Gardens. With directions to Bank and Beckton.

N

Bank ←

→ Beckton

━━━━ DLR on new infrastructure

═══ DLR on infrastructure of former rail lines

Miles
0   ½   1

RJD

The area has thus been transformed from its period of deprivation of rail facilities. It is a far cry from the Department of Transport's original idea that rail was not needed. More rail capacity is seen as essential to the successful development of the area and approval was at last given on 29th October 1993 for the extension of the Jubilee Line tube from Green Park via Waterloo, London Bridge, Bermondsey, Canary Wharf, Canning Town (where there will be interchange with the Beckton line) and on to Stratford.

The Government in 1992 transferred direction of the DLR from London Transport to the LDDC and called in management consultants. There had been much public criticism of DLR performance and service levels, but it must be remembered this was not only a railway employing new control systems, but one which was virtually being rebuilt from the moment it opened. The fault, as so often is the case, lay at the Government's door through short-sighted under-funding of a project that it now wants to privatise.

Facing Page **Bow Junction, where the London & Blackwall from Stepney joined the ECR (later GER) from Liverpool Street. The single line of the DLR is on the former up L&B track and the now singled connection on the down line diverges just beyond.** A.C. Mott

Below **Looking east over Minories in September 1989. The ramp up from the DLR Bank extension to Leman Street Junction is under construction to the right. To the left are the remains of Minories goods depot and approach viaduct. To the extreme left, a BR train approaches the site of Minories L&B station.** A.C. Mott

Grays–Upminster–Romford
Ken Frost

This important link between the market town of Romford, Tilbury and North Kent was completed in June 1893, no less than ten years after authorisation. K.A. Frost has made a special study of its story. Photos from the Author's collection except where otherwise shown.

Above **The 17.13 awaits departure for Upminster at Romford on 7th June 1954. It is headed by push and pull equipped ex-Midland 0-4-4T No.58062.** J.N. Faulkner

Facing Page **On 8th April 1910 4-4-2T No.28,** *Romford* **by name as well as destination, leaves Emerson Park Halt with a substantial train of six 4-wheeled coaches.** LCGB

The line between Grays and Romford, originating in the spirit of inter-company rivalry which characterised the railway history of the United Kingdom prior to 1914, was sanctioned by Parliament in preference to similar schemes promoted by the Great Eastern and also by an independent company, the Romford & Tilbury Railway. The London, Tilbury & Southend Railway's Act of 20th August 1883 contained an important clause giving that company running powers over 'so much of the Colchester line of the Great Eastern Railway Company as lies between the junction therewith by this Act authorised and the Romford station of the Great Eastern Railway together with the stations, watering-places, booking-offices, warehouses, loading-places, sidings, works and conveniences connected with the said portion of railway and station'. The period allowed for completion of the works was five years.

The LTS decided to apply to Parliament for an extension of time in respect of the Grays-Romford line, the Chairman having explained to a special meeting of the proprietors in January 1886 that their decision to do so was purely a precautionary measure as it was considered prudent to see how the traffic from the docks developed before they began work on the railway. There was a wide-spread conviction among the shareholders that the line would not pay but the Chairman warned that if they abandoned their powers the Great Eastern would be likely to step in immediately.

By the early part of 1889 the Directors had decided to go ahead with the project and had begun negotiations to acquire the necessary land. Within a few months, work had started under the superintendence of Mr J.R. Robertson, Resident Engineer, the Consulting Engineer being Arthur L. Stride, the London, Tilbury & Southend's General Manager. The contractors were J. Mowlem & Company of Westminster.

Work on the Grays–Upminster portion of the line was interrupted in February 1891 by a strike of wagon-fillers who were demanding an increase in their standard rate of pay from $4^{1}/_{2}$ to 5d per hour. Their hours were 6.30am to 4pm with one hour for meals and their regulation stint 16 wagons. Eventually some 220 men were involved in the stoppage — some of those reluctant to strike were threatened that they would be thrown into the River Ingrebourne if they did not do so! Operations were brought completely to a standstill for several days. The contractors contended that their men could earn 3s 9d per day whereas rates paid for similar work in other parts of the country varied from 3s 2d to 3s 6d per day. At that time the contractors' weekly wage bill for this particular line totalled about £500, rising to £800/900 in the summer months. Within a few days the strike collapsed and by the end of the year the Directors were able to forecast the early completion of this first section of the railway. It was duly opened for traffic on 1st July 1892 and was single track throughout with a passing loop at the only intermediate station, Ockendon. It had originally been intended to construct an embankment at Stifford where the track had to be taken over the Mardyke but instead a viaduct was later authorised by the Board of Trade and this was the principal engineering work on this section of the line.

Informal proposals were received by the LTS from the Great Eastern to the effect that the former company having built the line from Upminster to Romford should then lease it to them at 3% of its capital cost and that the LTS should also grant the Great Eastern running powers to Tilbury via Upminster and Grays. This suggestion which had emanated from Mr Parkes, Chairman of the GER was referred for consideration by the Board of the LTS to their Chairman, Manager and Solicitor whose report in October 1888 stated that the terms proposed by Mr Parkes did not afford a basis for negotiation.

By this time works on the Upminster–Romford section of the railway were in an advanced stage. Correspondence then passed between Mr Stride, the General Manager of the LTS and his opposite number at the GE, Mr Birt, concerning the alterations which would have to be made at Romford station to accommodate the former company's trains. Mr Birt thought it most undesirable that the LTS trains should run over part of the Great Eastern track into Romford station, 'a busy track especially in summer months which had many expresses running at a rate of 50mph over it' and after further negotiations an agreement was arrived at between the two companies.

The terms of this agreement provided that the LTS should build their own line into Romford and provide their own station at an estimated cost of £14,950 and pay the Great Eastern £100 p.a. as rent for the necessary land from the authorised junction of the Upminster branch to Romford station upon which land they should lay their own track, the Great Eastern to provide at their own expense accommodation for goods traffic to and from the LTS for a period of three years at the expiry of which each company was to be at liberty 'to exercise its Parliamentary rights so far as goods traffic was concerned' (this was a reference to the right of each company to bring up the question under the terms of Section 25 of The London, Tilbury & Southend Railway Act 1883). The LTS also agreed to give up the proposed junction with the Great Eastern main line.

As a result of the agreement a completely separate station was built at Romford with a frontage to South Street of 40 feet. A single platform was provided and a footbridge gave access to the up platform of the Great Eastern station which then had only two platforms. A new footbridge was erected between these two platforms by the Great Eastern to provide passengers with a means of access to or from either station without having to descend to street level. The 'Essex Times' was quite complimentary about this new station describing it as 'of neat and picturesque appearance and a great improvement to the town'. A physical connection was made five chains east of the platform between the Great Eastern up line and the LTS branch to facilitate the passage of freight traffic while at Upminster a small engine shed was built east of the station to house the locomotives which would be working the branch.

The Upminster–Romford section of the railway was opened for traffic on Wednesday 7th June 1893 without ceremony, the first train leaving Romford for Upminster at 6.58am headed by 4-4-2T No.5 'Plaistow' with Driver Saunders on the footplate. It was watched by groups of people congregated at windows and in almost every garden, the engine whistle being sounded repeatedly on the journey to mark the occasion. A number of officials travelled on this train — Mr James Robertson, Mr H. Poston (LTS Surveyor), Messrs Rowell and Higgins (Agents for the Contractors), Mr Jackson (Inspector of the works) and Mr Whitelegg (LTS Locomotive Superintendent).

The railway had been completed just in time for the Essex Agricultural Show which was held in Romford a week later. The initial service of trains was eight each way each weekday with three extra on Saturdays and five each way on Sundays. There were no intermediate stations on the Upminster-Romford section and apart from the passing loop at Ockendon the complete railway, Grays to Romford, was single track throughout. It was worked by Webb & Thompson's electric train staff system; the signalling installations were carried out by The Railway Signal Company of Fazakerley, Liverpool. At Upminster the Romford–Grays trains used the north face of the island platform on the down side, London passengers having to pass through the subway to gain access to the up platform.

In 1896 the LTS, exercising its rights under the agreement referred to above, opened a goods depot at Romford with an approach from Victoria Road. A considerable amount of goods traffic developed due mainly to the importance of Romford market, while a certain amount of coal was carried on the line in addition to traffic to and from Ind Coope's siding which was adjacent to the Great Eastern station. Some of the goods trains on the Upminster–Romford line were worked by the two 0-6-0 tender locomotives (Nos.49 and 50) acquired by the LTS but originally built for the Ottoman Railways.

Soon after the completion of the railway, a property developer from Dorset purchased 200 acres forming part of the Manor of Great Nelmes and 20 acres of the Manor of Lees Gardens, all situated within Hornchurch, and began the building of the Emerson Park Garden City estate, the first substantial development in modern Hornchurch aimed at the salaried middle class. Although this estate extended eventually up to the new railway at Butts Green there were no station facilities and travellers were obliged to make their way to Hornchurch or Romford stations. The necessity of walking 1½ or 2 miles in all weathers often entailed the negotiation of much mud in wet conditions and caused a good deal of inconvenience.

Eventually pressure built up among the residents of Emerson Park for the provision of a station and the LTS opened a platform at Butts Green on 1st October 1909 named

Emerson Park for Great Nelmes, but simply Emerson Park Halt on tickets. The 'Essex County Chronicle' commented 'October 1st will be a red letter day for the residents of Emerson Park Estate. The new station will be opened at Butts Green and a special service of trains will enable the hundreds of season-ticket holders to go to the city and back without the four-mile daily tramp or drive to and from Hornchurch station'.

In an attempt to capture a share of the traffic the Great Eastern immediately began a service of omnibuses between the new Halt and their Romford station to connect with their fast trains to and from the city. Two weeks later, however, the LTS provided a loop line on the north side of the running line some 500 yards north of Emerson Park Halt. This was to facilitate the reversal of trains at the latter point in order to channel traffic via Upminster rather than Romford. Season tickets from Emerson Park to Fenchurch Street were issued immediately the Halt opened at £2 17s 6d (£2.85) per quarter third class and £3 17s 6d (£3.85) first class.

The opening of Emerson Park Halt undoubtedly provided the incentive for the Great Eastern to expedite the opening of their new station at Squirrels Heath to serve the Gidea Park Garden Suburb then in course of development. This station was opened on 1st December 1910 and immediately a service of omnibuses was run on weekdays from Hornchurch, calling at Emerson Park Halt, to Squirrels Heath station in conjunction with Great Eastern trains. This service was confined principally to the morning and evening rush hours, the fare each way being 1d. For many years, even into LNER days, the station nameboards at Squirrels Heath carried the words 'ALIGHT HERE FOR GREAT NELMES' — a reminder of the Great Eastern's efforts to secure a share of the Emerson Park traffic.

The Midland takeover of the LTS in 1912 had relatively little effect upon the line. They did, however, give an undertaking that season ticket rates would remain unaltered for three years. At the absorption these rates from Emerson Park were as follows:-

TO FENCHURCH STREET,
STEPNEY or
BURDETT ROAD	1st CLASS			3rd CLASS		
	£	s	d	£	s	d
12 months	15	10	0	10	10	0
6 months	7	15	0	5	5	0
3 months	3	17	6	2	12	6

TO UPMINSTER
	£	s	d	£	s	d
12 months	1	10	0	1	0	0
6 months		15	0		10	0
3 months		7	6		5	0

The Midland made certain improvements to services, among them the introduction of cheap return tickets from Upminster and Emerson Park Halt to London every Thursday available by any train after 10 am. These fares were 2s 10d first class and 1s 3d third class. Also an extra train was provided from Upminster to Emerson Park in connection with the 12.10 night train from Fenchurch Street due at Upminster at 12.46am, by which passengers could reach Emerson Park at 12.54am. This had hitherto been a regular working on Saturdays only but was extended to Thursdays for the benefit of cheap return ticket holders who, incidentally, were allowed no luggage.

An early view of Emerson Park Halt. A train from Romford enters to pick up a reasonable number of passengers at a date prior to 1914.

An advertisement in the *Evening News* of 7th May 1908. Another advert in the same issue extolled 'charming country houses adjoining Upminster station at prices from £330'.

Services were maintained with little alteration throughout the First World War. As a result of agreements negotiated between the Midland Railway and Hall & Company Ltd of Croydon, sidings were put in at Romford between Brentwood Road and Victoria Road bridges. As the Midland era drew to a close due to the provisions of the Railways Act of 1921, there were 24 trains each way between Romford and Upminster on weekdays, nine of which were through services to and from Grays or Tilbury. In addition there were four reversals in each direction between Upminster and Emerson Park Halt (five on Saturdays).

The London, Midland & Scottish regime which took over on 1st January 1923 maintained similar services but the closure of that company's station entrance at Romford on 2nd April 1934 resulted from the LMS and LNE Pooling Scheme. Until then the use of the footbridge connecting the two stations at Romford had been restricted by gates which were kept locked when there were no Tilbury system trains in the station, there being no through fares between the Great Eastern and London, Tilbury & Southend via Romford. From now on this bridge was open at all times as all Tilbury line passengers had to use it to get to the LMS station.

By this time the District Line tracks had been extended from Barking to Upminster, the new services coming into effect on 12th September 1932, Upminster station having undergone extensive alterations. Until then the complete line — ie Grays–Upminster–Romford — had been worked as a through route but the new track layout at Upminster effectively severed it into two. From then onwards, the route was normally worked as two separate entities, although there were still some through services as connections continued to exist across the District Line until 1960.

In 1933 attempts were made by the Hornchurch Ratepayers Association to secure the provision of halts at Wingletye Lane, Hornchurch, and at Brentwood Road, Romford, due to the degree of housing development which had taken place, but without success. The LMS had by then announced their intention of carrying out tests with various power units on the Romford–Upminster line with a view to the operation of a shuttle service. On 11th July 1934 notice was given that push-pull units were to be put into service in addition to the ordinary trains and these started three weeks later. The introduction of these services rendered the run-round loop at Emerson Park redundant and it was removed in 1936. The junction with the LNER at Romford had been severed some five years previously and on 1st March 1936 the LTS signal-box which had stood at the end of the single platform at Romford was closed and removed.

Following the outbreak of the Second World War the strategic importance of the branch led to the restoration of the connection with the LNER east of Romford station. This occurred on 4th August 1940 with a new ground frame which would enable important dock traffic to be routed this way in the event of any interruption by enemy activity west of Upminster. Services on the route continued virtually unimpaired throughout the duration of the conflict but

Ockendon station in 1957. K.L. Cook

first class accommodation was abolished on 6th October 1941 in keeping with that on all local services within the London area. Eighty yards of track were destroyed on 30th June 1944 when a 'flying bomb' struck the nearby embankment close to Romford station.

In the aftermath of the war the summer timetable of 1946 showed 30 trains each way daily between Romford and Upminster on weekdays, the first leaving Romford at 6.46am and the last at 10.50pm. Two were through to Grays and a third ran to Tilbury with ferry connection at Gravesend. On Sundays there were nine trains in each direction between Romford and Upminster, five of which went through to Tilbury.

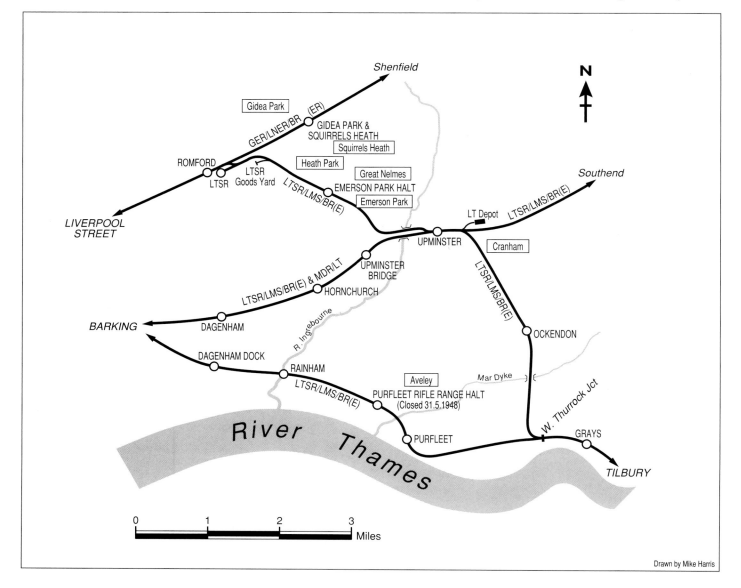

Drawn by Mike Harris

The 15.00 train from Romford arrives at Upminster behind 0-4-4T No.58065 on 1st October 1955. J.N. Faulkner

In February 1951, due to an acute fuel shortage on a national scale British Railways services throughout the country were subjected to many cancellations and modifications. Ten trains each way were cancelled on the Romford–Upminster line, three others relegated to Saturdays only and a further three each way were withdrawn except on Saturdays. As from 8th April 1951, the Sunday service was suspended entirely and was never renewed (apart from a very brief period in the following August). The southern section of the route was not affected.

The timetable with these reductions lasted until 17th September 1956 when diesel units took over from the steam operated services on the Romford–Upminster section only, whereupon train services were immediately doubled to 32 journeys each way daily from 6.05am until 9.22pm. Through running between Romford and Grays ceased at this time and since then each part of the route has been worked independently. As a result of the opening of the new London Transport depot at Upminster, the station there underwent certain alterations, the island platforms Nos.4 and 5 being allocated exclusively to London Transport trains and a new platform, No.6, being built on the north side of the cutting which was brought into use on 20th May 1957. Following removal of the crossing west of Upminster station on 4th May 1958, the Romford branch was left only with the connection via the Romford ground frame which was normally only in use for diesel sets proceeding to or from their depot at Stratford.

The Romford–Upminster part of the route was included in the Beeching proposals for withdrawal of services in 1963. Following a vigorous campaign led by the newly formed Romford–Upminster Branch Line Users' Association, backed by the local authorities and the MPs for the two constituencies of Romford and Hornchurch, the Minister of Transport refused to consent to closure. A further attempt to close the line was made by British Rail in 1969, the annual deficit being

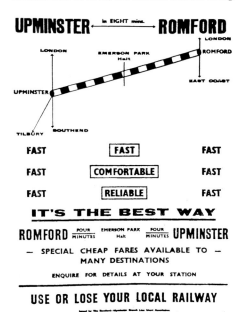

then quoted as £70,000. However, due to local efforts to publicise the line, earnings increased substantially from 1970 and it was considered that losses could be reduced still further by operating two-car sets so the Minister's decision, which was not finally arrived at until 1972, was that services should be retained. Freight traffic, however, was withdrawn, ceasing altogether following the closure of Romford Victoria goods depot on 4th May 1970.

On the Upminster–Grays section a large estate was built by the former London County Council at Aveley in the post-war period. An industrial estate was also built at South Ockendon and so this part of the railway, which in contrast to Upminster–Romford had remained predominantly rural, enjoyed a change of fortune from the 1950s onwards.

Following the provision of diesels on the Romford–Upminster section the trains from Grays used the up side bay platform at Upminster and continued to be steam hauled until diesel sets took over on 6th January 1958 providing a regular half-hourly service (hourly on Sundays) with a journey time between Grays and Upminster of 15 minutes. These trains crossed at Ockendon and there were some additional rush-hour services, some of which were through workings to Tilbury Riverside. Having regard to the traffic generated by the Aveley estate this southern section was included in the plans for the electrification of the former LTS, and four-coach electric sets began working on 17th June 1963. The electrification included the provision of a separate track from West

Passing trains at Ockendon on 30th November 1957 with 2-6-4T No.80132 heading the 12.46 for Tilbury Riverside. K.L. Cook

Thurrock Junction to Grays adjacent to the main line. This was installed in June 1959 and was, in effect, an independent extension of the Ockendon Branch.

On 24th December 1977 Ockendon signal-box was totally destroyed by fire and this resulted in the passing loop and its controlling signals being removed. In November 1978 new colour light signalling was installed at Ockendon and the passing loop reinstated, control passing to the signalman at Upminster. The final phase in the story of this cross-country line was the electrification of the Romford–Upminster section which followed many years later, electric services taking over on 12th May 1986 with a half-hourly interval on weekdays only.

The centenary of the opening of the Romford–Upminster line in 1993 was marked by the unveiling of a plaque in the booking hall of Romford station by retired booking-office clerk Mr Peter Ward. Present at the ceremony was British Rail's Great Eastern Divisional Director, Mr Bob Breakwell and local railway enthusiasts including several who had campaigned to keep the line open on the two occasions when its future was threatened.

The changeover to diesel. On 30th November 1957 ex-LTS 4-4-2T No.41978 passes Upminster East Box with the 11.00 working to Grays. At the same spot a diesel unit also for Grays was pictured on 27th October. K.L. Cook

The Waterloo & City Line
J.N. Faulkner

To its regular customers it has always been 'The Drain', but the Waterloo & City represents the culmination of the LSWR's effort to reach the City and for long was BR's only tube line. It has recently received its first new stock since 1940 and is now part of the London Underground. J.N. Faulkner takes a close look at the line's story.

Above **Original single unit motor car No.17 in the platform at Waterloo on 2nd September 1940 shortly before replacement.** British Rail

Right **1898 map of the route of the W&C showing the original authorised course of the Baker Street & Waterloo Railway.** Courtesy of the Railway Magazine

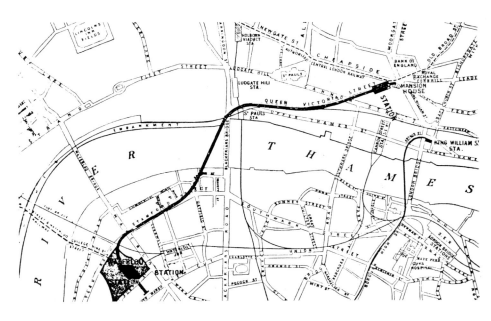

The W&C sidings and power house, with cars and the smaller electric loco laid bare about 1905 during the construction of the new Waterloo South Station. NRM

The LSWR's advance from Nine Elms to London Bridge had halted at Waterloo in 1848. From 1869 its passengers could cross the footbridge into Waterloo Junction station and take an SER train to Cannon Street, but the majority probably completed their journey to the City by bus or on foot. The opening of the City & South London Railway in 1890 showed the way for other deep-level underground links into the City. The Central London Railway soon secured powers in August 1891 for a line from Shepherds Bush to Cornhill, close to the Bank.

An underground railway would give the LSWR access to the City at a fraction of the cost of a surface line; according to *Railway Times* credit for this idea was due to the South Western's general manager, Charles Scotter. However, the line was to be promoted by an ostensibly separate company, the Waterloo & City Railway, though the five subscribers named in its Bill included Wyndham S. Portal (the then LSWR chairman) and Lt. Col Henry Campbell (his successor).

The Waterloo & City Bill was introduced into Parliament in January 1892, simultaneously with Bills for the Baker Street & Waterloo Railway and for a Central London Railway deviation from Cornhill to a station with public subways beneath the Bank road junction. The W&C Bill provided for a line one mile 47 chains in length from James Street in Lambeth to Mansion House Street in the City. Capital was to be £540,000 with borrowing powers for £180,000. The CLR Bill was

unopposed and had passed through all its stages when Parliament was dissolved in June 1892. The W&C Bill had only reached its second reading in the Commons and had therefore to be reintroduced into the new parliament in the 1892/93 session.

Among the objectors to the Bill was the SER — 'The W&C has been promoted in the interests of the LSWR who receive immense benefit from the SER Waterloo Junction to Cannon Street line without contributing to the cost of Cannon Street. The W&C is inconsistent with good faith on the part of the LSWR and a great injustice if it diverts traffic from a costly section of the SER'. Despite this feeling of outrage the SER withdrew its opposition in March 1893.

Clauses were inserted in the Bill to protect the Mansion House, 'a large and valuable building of great weight', *The Times* office in Printing House Square and the railway viaducts of the SER at Waterloo and the LCDR at Blackfriars as well as the District Railway tunnels there. Within the City no spoil from excavations was to be moved through the streets during the daytime and if any soil was dropped, the offending vehicles and horses could be seized in aid of the City Police Superannuation Fund. The Bill also granted powers for a working agreement with the LSWR and for that company to guarantee W&C dividend and interest payments. A period of five years for completion was allowed, with the W&C Act receiving Royal Assent on 27th July 1893.

The eight Waterloo & City directors held their first board meeting on 24th January 1894. Wyndham S. Portal became chairman with Colonel Campbell as his deputy; the remaining members of the board included two more LSWR directors and the general manager, Charles Scotter, and three other gentlemen, one of them giving his address as St. James's Palace. The company secretary was F.J. Macaulay and its solicitor S. Bircham & Co., both holding similar office on the LSWR. At its next meeting the W&C board appointed its engineers — W.R. Galbraith (the LSWR consulting engineer), R.E. Church and J.H. Greathead, the inventor of the tunnelling shield, replaced on his death in 1896 by the electrical expert Dr Alexander Kennedy from the firm of Kennedy & Donkin. The engineers were to be paid at the rate of 4% on cost, with £2,300 extra to Greathead for the use of his patents. In 1895 W.H. Preece joined them as Consulting Electrician at a fee of 500 guineas. The Resident Engineer on the work was H.H. Dalrymple Hay.

The prospectus for the company's share issue was published on 17th March 1894. At its head it stated that 'A Minimum Dividend of 3% will be payable out of Gross Receipts before any Deduction for Working Expenses is made by the LSWR company'. It continued — 'Having regard to the favourable situation of the W&C Railway, to the speed and punctuality with which it can be worked, to the rapid growth of the suburban traffic in the districts served by the LSWR and to the densely-populated district around Waterloo station, the directors confidently anticipate that the receipts will be much more than sufficient to meet the minimum dividend of 3%'. The working agreement with the LSWR provided for the latter to work the W&C at cost price (such cost not to exceed 55% of revenue). All surpluses after payment of working expenses and the guaranteed 3% dividend to be split two-thirds to the W&C, one-third to the LSWR.

The share issue closed on 21st March 1894, with 55,011 applications for the 53,000 £10 shares on offer. Among the 475 shareholders were such pillars of the City establishment as Sir Ernest Cassel and Sir Samuel Montagu. At a time when Consols paid around 2½%, a guaranteed minimum dividend of 3% was attractive to investors. Despite the presence of several LSWR directors on the original Baker Street & Waterloo board, the South Western offered only moral support to it and the promoters failed to raise capital. No W&C debenture stock was created until March 1898 when £60,000 was issued to the LSWR, followed by £10,000 more in June 1902.

Following the success of the share issue, the board proceeded to award the two separate construction contracts. The first was to cover the main running tunnels from Cross Street, near Waterloo, to the City including the Bank station. Of the seven tenders received, that of John Mowlem & Co for £229,064 was accepted on 5th April 1894. Construction of the station at Waterloo and of the connecting passages to the LSWR terminus formed the second contract. This involved prolonged consultation with the LSWR before detailed plans could be prepared and these were not ready until August 1895. This contract was offered to Perry & Co (Bow) Ltd, the LSWR's usual contractor for work at Waterloo; only if they refused would other tenders be invited, but a price of £108,608 plus £2,500 for initial maintenance was agreed in December 1895 and approved by the Board on 9th January 1896.

Completion of the Bank station required the co-operation of the CLR and of the City Corporation for W&C access to the planned subway system. Negotiations with the CLR commenced in April 1894, but it had difficulty in raising capital and only through the medium of an Exploration Company with mining interests able to attract foreign investors was the success of its share issue assured in June 1895. Agreement between the CLR and the W&C could then be reached in October 1895. According to the terms of the CLR's 1892 Act any other company having a station in the vicinity of the Mansion House could obtain access to its subways on payment of a contribution to their construction costs; the W&C's 50% share came to a total of £46,027. To this had to be added the £7,500 cost of the inclined passage linking its platforms with the subway system.

The W&C board felt that this arrangement was cheaper than building its own surface station at the junction of Queen Victoria Street and Bucklersbury, which would have involved expensive property purchase and the installation of lifts. Generations of City commuters trudging daily up 'The Drain', as they named the subway, came to regret the company's economy. In order to assist the completion of the W&C, the first sod for the CLR was cut at the Bank in October 1895.

To comply with the restrictions on excavations within the City, it was decided to construct the line from working shafts in mid-river, 236ft from the Surrey bank upstream of Blackfriars Bridge. J. Mowlem commenced pile-driving work for the staging on 18th June 1894 and by November the two shafts had been fully sunk and the first of four shields delivered, ready for boring to commence on 26th November on the up tunnel towards the City.

There had been some changes of plan at the Waterloo end of the line. The first choice of power station site had been on the south bank of the river, which could have been supplied by barge; later land in York Road on the north side of Waterloo was acquired but in June 1895

the board finally decided to locate the generating station and depot on the other side of Waterloo station in Aubin Street, off Lower Marsh, obtaining any additional land through LSWR powers. However, this site would require a hoist to the surface for rolling stock transfer and fuel supply on the York Road side of the terminus, connected to the North sidings. Planning at Waterloo was complicated by the successive changes in the route of the projected Baker Street tube, originally its depot was to have been on the Aubin Street site, next it proposed to terminate on the York Road side and share use of the W&C hoist and eventually the line was extended to Elephant & Castle with a depot at London Road, Lambeth.

The W&C Act specified two separate cast-iron running tunnels some 12ft in diameter, but slightly wider on curves. These were not parallel in the vertical plane — to assist acceleration the up line to the City left Waterloo on a 1 in 30 down gradient and after a level section under the river climbed towards Bank at 1 in 88. On the down line the corresponding gradients were 1 in 60 leaving Bank and 1 in 88 up approaching Waterloo. In mid-stream the roof of the tunnel was 23ft below the river bed. To avoid expensive property purchase the line swung away from Stamford Street towards the river on a sharp five chain curve and on the City bank turned at nine chains radius into Queen Victoria Street.

At Bank, approached through a scissors crossover, there were two 23ft diameter station tunnels with cross passages between the two 300ft platforms. Each platform track continued into tunnels housing lay-by sidings, although the down side extension had originally been intended as a low level subway to the CLR and was only equipped as a siding in 1900. Bank station was 59ft below the surface.

The Waterloo station was at right angles to the main line terminus and was built within four of its arches, whose foundations had to be deepened. The 310ft arrival and departure

The spartan interior of an original motor coach before the seats were upholstered. Commuters could occupy the journey by studying pictures of the scenery elsewhere on the LSWR.
Alan A. Jackson

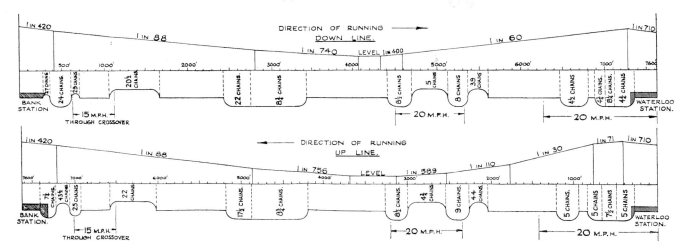

WATERLOO AND CITY LINE
DIAGRAM OF CURVES & GRADIENTS

platforms occupied separate arches, 17ft below ground level and 41ft below the main line tracks. Stairs and ramps linked the W&C platforms to all three sections of the LSWR terminus. The siding leading from the hoist made a trailing connection with the up line to the City at the point where the route curved round from beneath the station to follow Stamford Street. Beyond the platforms the tracks emerged into an open area, leading to a reversing siding, a lay-by road, two tracks for rolling stock maintenance and a line to the power station coal hoist.

Removal of spoil from the tunnel faces to the shafts was by light railway using two Siemens battery locos. After being raised to the surface, the material was carried by barge from the working stage to the Dagenham marshes. During the bitter winter of 1895 the Thames froze and work had to cease for over ten days — normally work was carried on continuously from midnight on Sunday to 6pm on Saturday.

Another interruption was caused by a Mr Farmer, with property in Southwark, who obtained an injunction against the W&C preventing them 'entering upon or under his premises'. Mr Justice Kekewich upheld the injunction in the Chancery Court and ruled in February 1895 that the W&C had been given no right in its Act to enter the property and should pay money into Court to meet any demand for compensation. Subsequently, tube railways paid easements to landowners for passage through their subsoil; at Waterloo the W&C paid £1,500 per annum to the LSWR for such use. More delay took place in March 1895, when the Metropolitan District Railway required the tunnelling beneath its line at Blackfriars to be done under compressed air. The installation of air locks interrupted progress towards the City for nine weeks. Compressed air working was also required on the South bank towards Waterloo through a thin layer of clay above loose gravel.

On 17th January 1896 the works were visited by the King of the Belgians, 'clad in appropriate costume'; it seems he was interested in a possible under-river tunnel at Antwerp. At this stage 2,835 yards of the 4,400 yards of running tunnel had been completed and work was about to start under Waterloo station. This required the underpinning of the

LSWR general offices and the excavation of the large brick-lined platform tunnels below the arches of the main line station. Work also started on the siding to the hoist and on the depot and power station site. At Bank, the second half of 1896 saw the construction of the large crossover tunnel followed during 1897 by the two platform tunnels.

By March 1897 the two running tunnels were finished, but the mid-river working shafts were retained for another year for the delivery of permanent way by barge from Nine Elms Wharf. The track was formed of standard LSWR 87lbs bullhead rail laid on longitudinal sleepers with a concrete base. Completion of access to the surface at the Bank was delayed by slow progress on the CLR's subway system; to enable the W&C to open in 1898 temporary staircases were provided at Walbrook and on the corner of Poultry. These were considered too narrow and steep by the Inspecting Officer, even after improvements had been made he required public access to be supervised during peak hours. Completion of all seven entrances to the subway system was not achieved until 30th July 1900 with the opening of the Central London.

The W&C Act prescribed the use of cable or electric traction. Having decided to generate its own electricity, one advantage of having the W&C power station at Waterloo was the ability to supply lighting power to the new main line terminus buildings in 1910. The generating station near Lower Marsh was equipped with five Davey Paxman boilers feeding six Bellis & Morcom engines, driving Siemens 200kw generators to produce 530 volts dc output, which was fed to a central conductor rail at a nominal 500 volts. Coal wagons for the power station were lowered down the Armstrong hoist to the branch siding and then worked by a small Siemens 4-wheel electric loco through the up platform to the depot yard and there hoisted up to the coal store. Siemens had won the contract for the electrical installation against seven other tenders at a price of £55,913.

During 1896 the W&C and LSWR had discussed the type of rolling stock to be used. With such a short line it was agreed that locomotive haulage would be inappropriate and in advocating motor coaches, W.H. Preece advanced the modern idea of having motors on

every car. In February 1897 the LSWR (who were to own the stock) asked the W&C to order 22 coaches on its behalf — 12 motors and 10 trailers. On 1st April 1897 tenders were received from six companies. The best delivery a British manufacturer could offer was eleven months, while for a comparable price, Jackson & Sharp of Wilmington USA quoted delivery to Southampton in seven months. So despite patriotic protest the £21,675 contract was awarded to them. The cars would be erected at Eastleigh carriage works and fitted with electrical equipment by Siemens at Waterloo.

The first batch of coaches reached Eastleigh on 28th October 1897. Completion of the Armstrong hoist in April 1898 enabled fitting out at Waterloo to be completed and trial running underground to commence in June. Rolling stock comprised five four-car trains, formed Motor-Trailer-Trailer-Motor, plus two spare motor cars. The two motor coaches were linked by power cables along the roofs of the cars (multiple unit working was still to come) and the large control wheel in each cab was not fitted with any 'dead man' device so that two men had to be present.

The timber-bodied cars carried the LSWR livery; despite the lack of scenery on the line, the 'padded cell' design of the C&SLR was not followed — a shareholder had suggested that travel should be as pleasant as on the new Budapest metro. Entrance was at the end of the cars with a guard in charge of each pair of gates. Forty-six passengers could be seated on wooden benches in the motor cars, 56 in the trailers. Later a thin covering of upholstery was added to the seats. Besides the small shunting loco (later numbered 75s), a large Siemens Bo.Bo. electric loco was provided as a spare and for emergency use in case of train failures; in 1915 this (now 74s) was transferred to the new LSWR power station at Durnsford Road.

The signalling system was devised by W.R. Sykes and J.P. Annett, the LSWR signalling superintendent. It was a form of lock and block with treadle bars, consisting of semaphore starting signals at each station and mid-river electric colour light advanced starting signals controlled by the station in rear. If the road was clear into the other terminus, the advanced starter was released and the main semaphore lowered at the starting station; if the other terminus was blocked only the calling-on arm was lowered. The intermediate signals also carried the colour light distants for the terminus in advance, with splitting signals for the two platforms at Bank. Having the intermediate signals in mid-river avoided trains having to re-start on the approach gradients. If any signal was passed at danger a contact wiper tripped the main power switch on the train. In later years the tunnel signals were repositioned for better visibility and the overlaps at termini reduced so that the intermediate signals could be operated as outer homes and the calling-on starters were then abolished.

Hopes of opening early in 1898 were not fulfilled and the line was not ready until July for Board of Trade inspection, the electrical equipment by Major F. Cardew on the 6th and the line itself by Major F.A. Marindin on the following day. The latter ruled that speed round the five chain curve should be limited to 10mph (soon this was relaxed to 15mph and later to 20mph), but the projected journey time of four minutes had been based on 25mph on the the curves and 35mph elsewhere. The revised running time of 5½ minutes made it impossible to provide the projected three minute service with the five trains available.

The official inauguration had been arranged for 11th July 1898 to mark the 50th anniversary of the opening of Waterloo station and was to be performed by HRH the Duke of Cambridge. The 80-year-old royal duke duly made a six-minute trip to the City and back, followed by lunch in the 'extensive' W&C booking hall at Waterloo. As with some recent royal openings of urban transport, the formal ceremony was not followed by the start of public services. Troubles with equipment affected the commissioning of the trains and deliveries were delayed by a strike in the engineering industry. A fire on 19th July within an arch at Waterloo damaged tiling and flooring in the passageways. Major Marindin revisited the City station on 27th July to approve the altered stairways. It was then hoped to open on 1st August, but not enough trains were available yet to maintain the service, though free rides could be offered to shareholders attending the half-yearly meeting on the 4th.

Public services at last commenced from 8am on 8th August with four trains at work and the fifth unit becoming available during September to form the spare train used during peak hours only. Services operated between 8am and 10pm on weekdays only with a five minute frequency during rush hours reducing to ten minutes off-peak. For some months there was continued electrical trouble with the trains and the LSWR board instituted a report book to record W&C incidents. Technical reports were submitted by eminent electrical experts — Lord Kelvin, Dr Kennedy and Sir William Preece. Siemens faced delays in obtaining spare parts and it was not until August 1899 that the W&C half-yearly report stated that the difficulties had been overcome. Another problem was the leakage of water into the tunnels at the Waterloo end; a sump at the lowest point collected the water and an additional electric pump was installed in 1900 to return some 100,000 gallons per day to the surface for use by the LSWR.

Tickets were issued at first from turnstiles at each station; the fares were 2d single and 3d return, trains being one class only, but after a year travelling conductors sold Bell Punch tickets on the trains. It was soon found that more frequent and more economical operation was needed during the off-peak period. Thus five double-ended single cars were ordered from Dick Kerr & Co in 1899 for delivery in late 1900. These seated 50 passengers and the guard could travel in the cab alongside the driver. Two more trailer cars were ordered in 1903 to cover overhauls or to form a sixth train at times of maximum traffic, using the two spare motor coaches.

The additional rolling stock required enlargement of the depot sidings to provide a total of seven tracks, now almost completely under cover, and this was done during 1903/4 as part of the LSWR's construction of its new South station. The W&C's original Electrical Engineer, M. Heap, was succeeded in November 1900 by his deputy, Herbert Jones, who in 1912 assumed the same office on the LSWR and presided over that company's electrification followed by that of the Southern Railway.

A paper given by Herbert Jones in 1905 stated that the daily average number of passengers was 17,592 and that Saturday was the busiest day. A four-minute service was operated during the rush hours, with the single cars providing a five minute frequency during the rest of the day. By 1913 the service was being closely tailored to the traffic — six-minute intervals from the 7am start until 7.30, then reducing to a maximum three-minute service between 9.20 and 9.56am when the bankers and stockbrokers arrived for the day's work, followed by a five-minute frequency for the rest of the day until the late evening brought a reduction again to six minutes. As the working company, the LSWR provided 41 traffic staff for the opening of the line, but motormen were not included in this total.

Passenger numbers slowly increased from 3,485,556 in 1899 to a maximum of 4,588,274 in 1902/3, but in addition there were numerous LSWR through season ticket holders. For its first three years of existence net revenue on the W&C was insufficient to meet the guaranteed dividend and the LSWR had to make up the difference. Late in 1900 the single cars began to reduce the cost of off-peak operation and at the same time, at the request of Sir Ernest Cassel, an electrical engineer, H.F. Parshall, submitted a report on improvements in working to the LSWR board in June 1901. Perhaps coincidentally, the working expenses for the second half of 1901 showed a decrease of £1,348 over the previous half-year and the W&C at last moved into profit. The proportion of working expenses to gross revenue fell to around 45% and this percentage became the fixed deduction from 1st July 1905.

The margin was still small and it would have been many years before the accumulated deficit of £11,907 due to the LSWR would have been repaid and for the W&C shareholders to receive anything above the guaranteed 3% dividend. It was found that the W&C had paid Siemens £20,099 for electrical equipment on the trains which should have been an LSWR charge. This was set off against the deficit and the W&C was now in a position to pay higher dividends, but for only four half-year periods during the W&C's independent existence did the payment reach 3¼%.

Increasing competition from the electrified District Railway, the tramcar and the motor bus threatened the LSWR's suburban traffic. Fare reductions might have to be made to meet the competition and the W&C would share any losses, thus ending any hope of increased dividends and, more seriously, raising the

possibility of the LSWR having to subsidise the guarantee again. In November 1905 the LSWR decided to obtain powers in its 1906 Bill to absorb the W&C. Terms for amalgamation were negotiated with Samuel Montagu, on behalf of the shareholders, and owners of £100 W&C Ordinary Stock were offered a choice of £67 LSWR Ordinary shares, £105 of 3½% Preference stock or £110 of 3% Debentures. The amalgamation was authorised by the Act of 20th July 1906 and was effective from 1st January 1907. W&C capital expenditure had totalled £606,551, financed by £540,000 Ordinary and £70,000 LSWR-held Debentures.

The construction of the low-level subway to the CLR was mooted during 1909/10, but was again deferred. The MDR in drafting its 1912 Bill offered to provide for an interchange station with the W&C at Blackfriars. Another link to the outside world might have resulted from the Metropolitan Railway's takeover of the Great Northern & City Railway in 1913. Hoping to make something of its isolated 3½ mile acquisition, the Met promoted a Bill for an extension from Moorgate to Bank, with the eventual possibility of converting the W&C to main line dimensions and connecting at Waterloo to the future electrified LSWR system — in fact to create a forerunner of Thameslink. These hopes foundered on the opposition by the Bank of England to any underground line near its vaults.

As a result of the LSWR's suburban electrification, from 1915 current for the W&C was supplied from the new generating station at Durnsford Road via a surface sub-station at Waterloo. Some of the plant in the old W&C power station was retained for stand-by use as well as to provide auxiliary supplies. In 1918 some relief to the weary 1 in 9 ascent from the

platforms at Bank was provided by inserting groups of steps at 40ft intervals to reduce the gradient.

The return of peace brought serious overcrowding to the W&C, despite its first fare increase since 1898. At the LSWR's 1920 annual meeting, shareholders complained that during the morning rush hour around 2,000 commuters would be waiting to join trains at Waterloo and one would have to wait for the fourth or fifth train to be able to get on board. In 1921 the line carried 8,683,000 passengers and was running 428 trains daily, compared with 380 in 1913. As a result of these complaints Sir Herbert Walker proposed to the LSWR board in February 1920 to acquire six new all-steel trailers to lengthen the six existing trains to five cars. The electrical equipment on the motor coaches would be replaced to secure better acceleration with the longer trains, providing 24 trains per hour instead of 20 and offering 102 seats per minute instead of 68.

A year later the board came to a revised decision to build instead four trailers of the original design, which with one of the two existing spare vehicles would provide five trains of five cars, with one car in reserve. Without additional power the longer trains would be slower and this was recognised by the inspecting officer Major G.L. Hall in November 1921 when approving consequent changes to the signalling. The LSWR's reluctance to spend large sums on improving the W&C may have been due to Sir Herbert Walker's expressed hopes at this time for a full size tunnel to link the suburban routes into Waterloo via the City to the SECR lines near London Bridge, soon to be electrified by the SR.

An additional trailer car, Eastleigh built, passes Esher en route for Waterloo behind an Adams 4-4-0 No.686. L&GRP

The shortcomings of the W&C were raised at the SR's annual meeting in 1930 and powers were included in its 1931 Act for a new subway and a double escalator at the Bank. Although the signalling limited the service to 20 trains per hour, the additional coaches on the 428 daily trains provided 1,316 daily car journeys compared with 1,076 in 1921, conveying 9,800,000 passengers in 1937.

In February 1938 a deputation of regular travellers extracted the admission from the SR chairman that he was ashamed of the condition of the line. In conjunction with the LPTB, plans were prepared for a triple escalator at Bank and low-level interchange subways to the other tube lines, powers being obtained in the SR's 1939 Act. The modernisation package also included resignalling the line and new rolling stock. Meanwhile the patience of travellers was still asked for.

The outbreak of the Second World War prevented any construction at Bank, but work continued on installing automatic colour light signalling with a small semi-automatic panel at Bank station. The conductor rail was moved to the usual SR outside position to supply the standard 600 volts. New trains had been ordered from English Electric — 12 motor cars and 16 trailers to form 5 five-car units for peak period use, plus three spare vehicles. The motor coaches were double-ended and could run singly during the off-peak hours. Each five-car train provided 236 seats and could accommodate some 600 passengers under rush-hour conditions. The new stock was delivered during 1940 and the line was closed between 25th and 27th October for the changeover and resignalling to take place. This was achieved despite nightly visits by the Luftwaffe and the line was reopened on 28th October, when the City terminus was officially renamed as 'Bank'.

The modernised W&C had hardly settled into service, when at 10.45pm on 8th December a large bomb penetrated the roadway opposite Waterloo's Victory Arch and broke the crown of the down line tunnel for 30ft, filling the crater with rubble and flooding the line with 1½m gallons of water. Removal of the debris and rebuilding of the tunnels was a slow process and it was 3rd March 1941 before a partial service was restored, with normal working from 15th April. Two days later,

1940 motor coaches Nos.62 and 61 in platform 1 at Bank station on 5th September 1981. Two-car trains provided off-peak services for a period after single-car operation had ceased. C.J. Marsden

bombing near Waterloo sub-station interrupted power supplies to the W&C and a limited service was provided using LPTB current. On 19th April the line was closed temporarily while the Royal Navy carried out mine-sweeping operations in the Thames. The conflagration in the arches below Waterloo following the bombing of 10th May, closed the terminus and filled the W&C with the water poured on the fire. Within the City, unexploded bombs lay near the line in Queen Victoria Street and Walbrook; the latter was not removed until 22nd May, allowing the tube to reopen on the 26th. The W&C had never operated on Sundays until the need to cater for servicemen on leave crossing London was met by an evening service between 7th March 1943 and 23rd February 1947.

Steam traction made its only appearance on the W&C on 13th April 1948, when M7 0-4-4T 672 fell into the Armstrong hoist while shunting and had to be cut up on the spot. The 1939 plans for escalators at Bank were reconsidered in 1950 and again in 1955, when consultants came up with the alternative idea of an inclined travolator, which was approved in March 1957.

This had the advantage of moving passengers towards their destination and by being built on the site of the up line extension siding could allow the existing slope to be retained during construction and then to carry downward traffic during the morning peak when both of the Otis travolators would be running upwards. These rose 42ft on a 1 in 7 gradient and could carry 10,000 passengers per hour. The main contractor was Mitchell Bros & Co and the engineer was, appropriately, Mr L.A. Drain. The old 'Drain' subway was relined and the station platforms were raised and reconstructed in concrete as part of the project, which was opened officially by the Lord Mayor on 27th September 1960. The 1980s refurbishment of Waterloo included new tiling and platform surfaces to brighten up the gloomy W&C station tunnels.

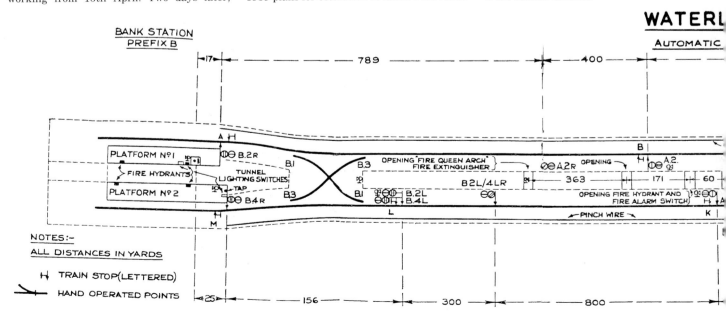

The journey to Waterloo, 1971 version. On 19th June a motor coach and trailer pass Surbiton in the charge of Class 33 loco No.6518. J.N. Faulkner

Major overhauls of W&C stock had traditionally been done at Eastleigh or Lancing, but from 1972 Selhurst depot took over this work. In 1985/86 sidings 1-3 at Waterloo were converted into a two-road maintenance depot able to carry out all routine work on W&C stock. The 1940 vehicles were gradually modernised — plastic interiors in 1960, blue instead of green livery together with silver ends, doors and roofs in 1971, fluorescent lighting, blue upholstery and NSE livery in 1987, partly financed by £150,000 sponsorship from Allied-Lyons. Some refurbishment was done at Swindon, but two cars in bad condition were withdrawn from service in 1982, followed in 1986/87 by three more cars which lingered in Waterloo North sidings until these had to be cleared for the construction of the new International station. This project also involved the removal of the Armstrong lift so that the W&C had to carry on with the surviving 50-year-old vehicles already underground. The shunting loco (DS75) had been

pensioned off in 1969 and has found a home in the National Railway Museum as an example of early electric traction technology.

Services have become increasingly unreliable in recent years. Four train operation in peak hours became the norm from 4th October 1982, though sometimes only the operating minimum of three trains has been available. When a water main burst in Lower Marsh on 23rd November 1975, the depot and tunnels were flooded, swamping all the trains and two months elapsed before full services were resumed. There have also been periods of staff shortages and of industrial action by the notoriously militant South Western drivers. Since 14th September 1963 Saturday services have ceased at lunchtime and eventually were worked by one train running at 15 minute intervals. During engineering work this frequency could be maintained on a one-train-in-current basis using one track in both directions. Off-peak single car working had already ceased.

Through tickets were issued via the W&C to a limited number of Underground destinations. Ticket issue on the trains had been replaced in 1940 by booking offices at each terminus, which gave way during the 1960s to automatic machines. Tickets to Bank were collected on entry at Waterloo, other tickets were clipped, but this barrier was abolished during the 1980s and travelling inspectors were supposed to charge a 'Standard Fare' for ticketless travel which was a forerunner of the Penalty Fare system. Soon the W&C had become part of the LT Zonal fare structure and tickets could be obtained from the Underground booking offices.

Below **Track and signalling plan following the 1940 modernisation.** British Rail

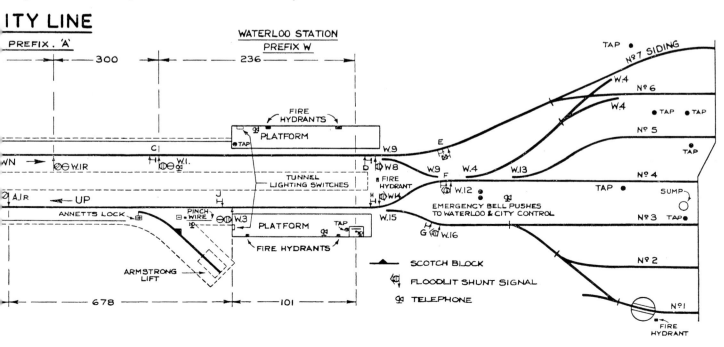

The W&C has always been an extreme example of the South East's peak hour problem. In 1960 84.7% of its 41,200 daily users travelled during the peak, 53.6% of them in the two busiest hours. Patronage had fallen to 31,500 per day in 1982, but half still travelled during these two hours. Following the City's 'Big Bang', traffic recovered with 37,000 passengers using the line's 340 daily trains in 1989, but only 37.2 per cent of them during the two busiest hours, perhaps reflecting the changes in the financial world's working pattern. Recession and service interruptions subsequently reduced the daily traffic to fewer than 27,000 passengers in 320 trains during 1992. Peak hour operation at Bank was assisted by step-up working with a turnover crew ready to take the train back to Waterloo without waiting for the incoming men having to fight their way along the crowded platform to change ends. The commuters were trained to form queues at points on the platform opposite each carriage door; during the 1980s refurbishment of the stations these spots were marked by incorporating the NSE stripes in the tiled edging.

Replacement of the 1940 stock was the subject of prolonged consideration. The Docklands Light Railway was being extended to Bank, but with incompatible rolling stock. Interchange with the W&C could however be achieved by building the long-delayed low level subway. Any novel ideas for new forms of traction were discarded in November 1989 in favour of a £23 million scheme to acquire five new four-car trains of the design being built by BREL/ABB for the LUL Central Line and to modernise the power and signalling systems to the latest LUL standards. The new cars are longer than the 1940 stock and this has required tunnel clearances to be eased round the curves at Blackfriars and over the Bank crossovers. The central conductor rail has been restored to conform to LUL's four-rail system.

To provide more working time, the Saturday service was withdrawn in June 1991 and weekday closure was brought forward from 10pm to 8.30pm in the autumn of 1991. The W&C was closed completely between 8th August and 6th September 1992, mainly to replace waterlogged longitudinal sleepers in the tunnels and to make alterations in the depot to accommodate the new stock. The W&C closed again from 29th May 1993 to enable the old stock to be replaced by the new trains, the exchange being made by crane via a new opening to the depot area off Lower Marsh. This was followed by the commissioning of the new trains and signalling system, incorporating ATO and ATP supervised from a control centre at Waterloo.

The reopening of the Waterloo & City on 19th July 1993 was accompanied by the restoration of a Saturday service until 18.00 and the operation of a three minute interval during the morning peak period, which now commences soon after half past seven. However teething troubles with signalling and trains caused frequent interruptions.

The Waterloo & City has thus lost many of its unique features and as a result of the first stages of BR privatisation it has become part of London Underground. But, with its third generation 'state of the art' equipment, it will be ready for a second century of service.

Right **Halfway through the changeover, trains of 1940 and 1992 stock can be seen side by side in the depot. Note the brand new fourth, negative, rail.** C.J. Marsden

Half-century old refurbished motor coach No.61 in Network livery in the re-equipped depot at Waterloo on 6th September 1992. C.J. Marsden

In May 1993, during the changeover, one of the new cars is lowered into the depot through the 'hole' alongside the cab roadway from Lower Marsh. On the end of the car is a 'W' sticker to ensure that this was the 'Waterloo' end, as mistakes could not be rectified. C.J. Marsden

Roger St Clair and
Tony Endersby

Signalling the Dover Triangle

The authors record the railway
scene at Dover immediately prior
to the opening of the Channel
Tunnel and trace the history of the
signal boxes in the area.

In the heyday of the railways, with thousands of staff, drivers, firemen, porters and signalmen, just to name the 'front line', it wasn't unusual to have a large number of railway related buildings in a small area. There could be engine turntables and sheds, coaling stages, traincrew offices, shunters' lobbies as well as the usual platform buildings, including signal boxes: all the paraphernalia of a busy working railway.

In 1893 for instance, to come upon four signal cabins in the space of a mile and a half would not be thought of as unusual in and around a large city. In London the boxes could be named, as Clapham 'A', Clapham 'B' and 'C', plus Clapham Yard. Similar named boxes at Liverpool, Manchester or some other large city would be quite normal. Four working signal boxes close together in a small town might seem extravagant. Four fully working boxes, staffed for 24 hours a day, 364 days of the year in a small town in the mid-1990s would appear an anachronism. Even more odd, as a box number five has not long closed.

The four signal boxes to which I refer are in the town of Dover. Ah yes! I can almost hear you say, but it *is* a very busy port. True, but there is not a railway near the main port, which is situated in the eastern part of the town. The four boxes are situated a good way from the main docks and they are all within 1½ miles of track. Were it not for an intervening short tunnel, the signalmen could almost see each other working.

At the beginning, two separate railway companies ran their services into Dover. First to arrive via the unusual Shakespeare tunnel was the South Eastern Railway. This line ended as a terminus on the western outskirts of Dover. The line, after leaving the twin portals of Shakespeare tunnel, ran over a wooden viaduct built directly onto the pebble beach, the very same beach used by those stalwarts of the sea, the cross-channel swimmers.

It is perhaps worth noting in these days of fast food outlets, that this rather primitive station with its two wooden platforms, and the first station to be built in Dover, had two refreshment rooms, one on each platform, when it opened in 1844.

The station was surprisingly named Dover Town: it wasn't anywhere near the town but near the sea. It boasted an engine shed, turntable and two carriage sidings. In those early days 'signalmen' as such didn't exist and it was some years before the pointsman or 'Bobbie' was housed in his own little hut. It was over 20 years before two cabins were built at Dover Town, Dover 'A' and 'B'.

Later when the old wooden viaduct was removed and a brick and concrete structure was built, the carriage sidings were extended and a small marshalling yard added. At this time a third signal box was added, the yard box. The time now had slipped forward to 1880. Those original boxes didn't last long and by the end of the eighties all three boxes were pulled down and a new one built. The only bit of railway left from those far off days is the down platform now called the military dock; a left-over from when troops were stationed at Archcliffe Fort.

In the late 1850s another railway was scheduled to end at Dover, The London Chatham & Dover, or as it was irreverently called after a few years, The London Smashem & Turnover Railway. In 1861 the new railway arrived via three tunnels into the heart of Dover and in 1863 a second terminus station had been built and named Dover Town and Harbour. This line finished only 300 yards from the SER Dover Town station. It must have seemed even then that the two lines ought to join up.

The LCDR station had an all-over roof, a footbridge and a central engine release road. It remained a terminus for only three years before the line did at last join up with the SER. One of the platform buildings is still in evidence today. For some years it was used by H.M. Customs as a bonded warehouse. At the time of writing the building is empty and the new dual carriageway into Dover just misses it. I believe it is now a listed building. The first signal cabin was built in 1867 and was a crude building with a leaky roof. This box remained until 1880 when it was superseded by another which was better and bigger. This second box lasted until 1934 when the present cabin was built, and is the second of the Dover four in action this present day. The box is now known as Hawkesbury Street Junction. An interesting feature of the one remaining station building is a brick tower or chimney-like structure on the end of it. It used to be a beacon for ships at sea. Today the top part of the tower is missing.

In 1850 two important things occurred in Dover. The first was that the construction of a large hotel was started very close to Dover Town station for the comfort of passengers on the SER who might wish to be put up in the town before or after their cross-channel trip. The second thing was that the town bigwigs had decided that the old wooden pier dock would soon become inadequate and a new one should be built.

In a short space of time and with a foresight not usually noticed in such worthies, they matched words with actions and plans were drawn, passed and money raised and work started in the following year. That same year the new hotel was finished and named 'The Lord Warden'. Soon after this, the new passenger ferry pier was finished and named Admiralty Pier.

In 1861 SER trains began to run on to the Admiralty Pier and almost at once the LCDR complained that the SER now had an unfair advantage. Again the SER could take their passengers right to the boat, as the line from Dover Town went right on to the pier. Passengers alighting at the new Harbour station on the LCD had to walk all of 300 yards for their boat.

Fortunately for all concerned, in 1861 the Dover Harbour Board was formed and one of the first jobs that it turned its hands to was to get the LCDR to connect to the new Admiralty Pier. In 1864 this was accomplished to everyone's satisfaction, and all was peace again.

Four years later on 1st March 1868 a murder was committed at Harbour station. The station master, one Edward Walsh, had an argument with a porter named Thomas Wells over, it is believed, overtime working. Wells went home and returned with a gun and shot the luckless Walsh dead. Wells was arrested, tried and found guilty of murder and remanded in Maidstone prison to await the death penalty. On 10th August of the same year at 10.30am he was hanged.

In 1881 a 16 chain connection was opened between Hawkesbury Street Junction and Archcliffe Junction on the SER, while wooden platforms on the new line were provided as part of Dover Town station. The severe curvature of the spur still imposes a 10mph speed limit. It was jointly owned by the SER and LCDR and completed a triangle between the other two lines which converged on the Admiralty Pier from Hawkesbury Street and Archcliffe Junctions.

Leaving Harbour station in the Canterbury direction, the railway immediately enters a 684 yard long tunnel called, by chance, Harbour tunnel, on the top of which were housed soldiers in a large barracks. The barracks are now gone and only few ruins of buildings are left. On the Canterbury side of the tunnel were some other ruins. These were very much older and were of St Martin's Priory. Near to this spot the LCDR passed and on it a station, Dover Town, was built and opened on 22nd July 1861. With the completion of Dover Town & Harbour station in 1863, the 1861 station was renamed Priory. A fair size yard was built at Priory, which also had a four-road double-span roofed engine shed and a turntable. A little later a large water tower was constructed which is still standing today. In the early thirties the yard, station and sidings were remodelled almost out of recognition, and the motive power depot moved to the shore west of Dover Town.

In keeping with some other main line stations on their route, the company built a subway in place of the usual overbridge. However, half way through the work a large burial site was struck. Centuries of bones descended onto the hapless diggers, who soon packed up. After some consultations with local religious figures it was decided to fill in the site and construct an overbridge.

Ex-LCDR Class R 0-4-4T No.A668 passes the Lord Warden Hotel as it approaches Dover Marine with a down local in September 1924. F.J. Agar/Pamlin Prints

At the turn of the century the Dover Harbour Board decided to construct the Prince of Wales Pier. A temporary station was built on it and a lead-off from Harbour Station was provided. As the latter could only be taken half way down the main line and the down platform was already in situ, the engineers made the last third of the down platform at Harbour station to swivel on wheels. The lead-off ran off under the platform. The train would pull down to the seaside end of the down platform, the top third would swivel round and the train would, with a tank engine on the front, pull out for the Prince of Wales Pier.

The finished line, pier and swivel platform were all working by 1902, the line passing very close to the Holy Trinity Church. The Reverend James Daniels was incensed by this and wrote to the company saying that the trains were disturbing his worshippers. After some initial wrangling the priest accepted £30 per annum disturbance money.

At the other side of the tunnel at Dover Priory the signalmen were complaining that the box as built some 30 years before was too small, as the frame stretched end to end of the box and the last two levers each end almost touched the wall. They would have to wait another 25 years before a new box was built. It was constructed in 1930 and is the third of the four remaining boxes working Dover to this day.

Over on the Admiralty Pier all was not well. Passengers waiting for trains or boats had very little shelter from the elements. Apart from the two platforms in tandem, the only other structure was a brick wall. In bad weather when the sea was rough, the waves would pour over the platform and bounce off the wall, and the passengers and their luggage would become a trifle damp. About 1900 someone had the idea that the prevailing conditions could be rectified with a canopy covering the platform. It was then suggested that the station should be made bigger. In 1907 the Harbour Board took over Admiralty Pier, leasing it to the LCDR. Plans were drawn up for a large covered station, with two island platforms. Twelve acres of land were reclaimed from the north east side of the Admiralty Pier and this put the passengers a little further away from the sea and its unpredictable moods.

However, for once things went very slowly. The plans were held up, money wasn't forthcoming and it seemed touch and go for some time. Then everything was settled about who would pay for what and where; and building commenced. As 1913 drew to a close, work was well under way and the covered station roof was taking shape, as was the maze of point work at the station throat which had three lines from Harbour station and three from Dover Town. The future for overseas travel looked bright. Unfortunately the feeling in Europe was far from bright and before the new station was opened in 1914, war had been declared. The station was called the Marine and was used for military traffic only until 18th January 1919 when it was finally opened to the general public.

The small but tall minaret-looking signal box that worked the line on the Admiralty Pier was pulled down in 1914 and a large new and double-manned box was built. Search as I may I can find no record of the date of the first box, but I would think probably about 1870. The Marine box is now single-manned and works to this day. As one new station opened, an old one closed. The first station to be built in Dover, Dover Town, closed on 14th October 1914.

The Lord Warden Hotel was refurbished as the twenties began and the railways of Kent amalgamated into the Southern. Now we had the heady days of The Golden Arrow boat trains and along with the beginning of the new so we had an end to the old. In 1927 Harbour station closed along with its unique swinging platform and the tram road to the Prince of Wales pier and its draughty station. In 1934 the old Harbour box was knocked down and a new one built on the other side of the tracks where the down platform had been; it was named Hawkesbury Street box and is another of the boxes working today. It is of the early type of design employed by the Southern Railway; the most distinguishing feature of which is the half timber, half brick eaves on the end walls. Today the windows have been replaced by modern sash ones and the original locking room windows have been bricked up.

Also in the late twenties, a large shunting yard was planned, along with customs sheds and shunters' lobbies. A large lock was completed to take train-ferries. At one end of the lock was a 'link span', a draw bridge contraption that lowered a ramp down onto the ship. Two railway lines on the span corresponded to two tracks on the ship. The loading and unloading was got down to a fine art; two engines in steam 'pulled' the boat train, or went up the ramp together so as not to unbalance the ship. Wagons were loaded and unloaded this way. The yard was at the back of the now defunct Harbour station, and by the time it was demolished and the new Hawkesbury Street box was finished, the yard and lock were under completion. Many problems were overcome before the span and the yard were open to traffic in 1936. The lock was a necessity, as tidal flow in Dover can be as much as 27 feet. Across the top of the span another box was opened and named Ferry box. This box closed on 8th October 1974.

Dover Marine station, now known as Dover Western Docks, with 'Battle of Britain' Class 4-6-2 No.34071 *601 Squadron* on an up boat train via Faversham.
Rev A.W.V. Mace

Controlling the third apex of the triangle, outside Western Docks Station and today rather remote from the remaining lines into the station, is Dover Marine signal box. Class L1 4-4-0 No.31758 running light from Dover shed to Priory Station passes the Marine signal box in April 1959. R.C. Riley

Rebuilt Stirling Class O1 0-6-0 No.31434 shunting vans at Dover Marine, 4th April 1959. This engine was withdrawn four months later. R.C. Riley

Three of the four boxes remaining in use at Dover, namely Hawkesbury Street Junction, Archcliffe Junction and Dover Marine, retained Absolute Block Working into 1994. Note that although the station at the Marine was renamed Dover Western Docks some time ago, the signal box is still called Dover Marine. This is one of the very few places left in the country where there is a separate signal box at each corner of a triangle. Not only that but shunting and Trip movements between these three boxes are permitted.

It may seem strange that there is this isolated patch of Absolute Block Working. The reason is that it was decided when converting the adjacent areas to Track Circuit Block that it would be better to leave Block working in force here because a signalman could lock himself up in a Panel Box. The distances between the junctions are very short and 12-car trains on each leg of the triangle would overlap each other. This is not to say that this problem cannot arise with Block Working — 'Locked round the Block', as it is called, but it can more easily be put right with this method of signalling.

To start with we will look at Hawkesbury Street Junction. The lever frame is a Westinghouse A2 one which became along with the A3 frame the Southern's standard frame. It has 80 levers but 55 of them are now spare. The Block Instruments are Standard 3 Way to Archcliffe and the Marine. Bells only are used to and from Dover Priory as Track Circuit Block regulations apply to the Priory. Instead of the usual bell plungers to operate the block bell there are tappers which are much easier to use, as it is possible to rattle out the codes much more quickly than can be done with a plunger. To send the codes quickly, though, is probably not what the authorities have in mind! Because of the length of the frame there are repeater bell plungers at the opposite end of the block shelf to which the bell and tapper are situated.

The bell codes are the standard ones for trains proceeding to Archcliffe and the Priory which are taking the Faversham route, and Special Code List No.1 for trains to Dover Western Docks and to the Priory which are taking the road to Martin Mill and Minster. Special Code List No.2 is used for trains going into the Ferry Sidings from the Priory. Unfortunately, the Ferry Sidings are not now used a great deal other than for trip workings and little traffic goes in direct from the Priory. Trip shunts to and from the Marine and Archcliffe are permitted on the Right Road.

All the signals are three-aspect colour lights and the points are motor worked. Shunting signals are of the position light variety. 52 and 55 levers are control levers and release Priory's 47 and 45 starting signals and Archcliffe's shunt signal No.25 protecting movements from Archcliffe towards the Box on the Down Road respectively. There is full track circuiting.

Interior views of, from top to bottom, Dover Marine signal box in 1989 and Archcliffe Junction and Hawkesbury Street Junction in 1991. Tony Endersby

The method of working is as follows. When a train on the Down line is described by the Priory it is immediately offered to Archcliffe if it is going towards Folkestone and Ashford and when accepted the relevant signal is cleared. If the train is going to the Marine, then it is not offered to the Marine until it is leaving the Priory. The reason for this is to avoid keeping road traffic waiting too long at the barriers controlled by the Marine Box. When a train arrives at the Priory, a Train Approaching light is illuminated and when it leaves the Priory station a klaxon sounds in the Box to warn the signalman that it has left. In the Up direction trains can be accepted from the Marine and Archcliffe at the same time. Immediately a train is offered from either of these two boxes it is described on the bell to the Priory. Trip workings out of the Ferry Sidings (now known as No.2 and No.3 Sidings) towards the Marine or Archcliffe are usually shunted out onto the Down Road (after Blocking Back 3-3 to the Priory). Trip movements going into these sidings are sent towards the Priory after giving the appropriate Shunting into Forward Section bell (3-3-2) and then sent back through 11 and 14 points. Thereafter 8 is sent to the Priory withdrawing the Shunt movement to the Box in advance. Wrong Line movements can be taken from Archcliffe.

Archcliffe Junction is on the south western leg of the triangle and looks after the junction of the line from Folkestone to Hawkesbury Street and the Marine. It also controls the western end of the Up Yard. Oddly enough, the Track Diagram depicts the Yard as a single siding which appears to terminate at buffer stops, whereas a series of sidings go past the cabin and have an eastern exit looked after by the Marine Box.

The lever frame is a South East & Chatham one of 40 levers; seven being spare. A number of signals work semi-automatically, that is, 1, 3, 5, 35 and 36. Track Circuit Block Regulations apply to Folkestone East using Magazine Train Describers with bell communication for emergency use. To Hawkesbury Street and the Marine standard three-way Instruments are installed. Standard bell codes are utilised between the Box and Dover Marine and to Hawkesbury Street for trains taking the Faversham line and terminating at Dover Priory. Code List No.1 is used for trains taking the Martin Mill route. It is the usual practice to offer a train to the Marine or Hawkesbury Street when BM Track is occupied, which is inside Shakespeare Tunnel. Trains cannot be accepted from both Hawkesbury Street and the Marine at the same time because of the short distance between the Home signals and the junction points. Also, a train must not be accepted from Hawkesbury Street until the junction points — No.24, have been reversed. Furthermore to protect shunt moves towards the Marine and Hawkesbury Street, 25 shunt signal is slotted by Marine's lever EDB 100 and Hawkesbury's lever EDJ 55. Trips can be made on the Right Line to and from the other two boxes on the triangle and Wrong Line moves can be made to and from the Marine but only to Hawkesbury Street. The bell codes used for these movements are 3-3-1 for freight trips (3-3-2 for shunt movements) in the Up direction between this Box and the Marine & Hawkesbury Street, and 1-3-3 for freight trips in the Down direction between this Box and the Marine and Hawkesbury Street. If a Wrong Line trip is to take place then the following procedure is undertaken where these moves are permitted: 3-3-1 or 1-3-3 is sent to the Box in advance. This bell is acknowledged by sending 2-3-3 (the Wrong Line bell code) to Archcliffe which acknowledges this bell. After the Wrong Line move is completed, Archcliffe receives the bell 5-2.

Wrong Line moves are allowed towards Folkestone East on the Down Road as far as ZE3 signal after a clear understanding has been reached with the Folkestone signalman and when there is no train on the Down line between Folkestone's YE11 signal and Track Circuit BU situated to the west of the Martello Tunnel.

To complicate matters even more, Down trains to Hawkesbury Street become Up trains when they pass this Cabin and Down ones become Up trains, which means that the signalman has to make sure that he sends the right shunting or trip bell code when these movements are to take place between this Box and the Marine or Hawkesbury Street. As can be seen from the above, movements going towards the Marine are Down shunts when made on the Right Road, but are Up movements when they are towards Hawkesbury Street on the Right Road.

Three fences are situated along the cliffs to protect the railway from falls of chalk. As soon as these fences are fouled an audible and visual alarm is given in the Box and the appropriate signals return to red. If Fence No.1 is fouled, then signals A364 and 3 go to danger, Fence No.2 returns 3, 5 and 35 and Fence No.3 returns 1, 3, 5, 35 and 36. The signals can only be reset after the blockage has been cleared and then by special keys at Re-Set panels.

Of all the boxes built by the SE&CR, Dover Marine was not only the largest in terms of size of frame but also the biggest in size.

Only 48 of the 112 levers are in use today. The frame is an ex-SE&CR one and was probably built specially for this Box. The Block Instruments are three-way Closed Block to the other two cabins — Hawkesbury Street Junction and Archcliffe Junction. The Bell Codes used are the standard ones to Archcliffe, and to Hawkesbury Street for trains taking the Faversham route, and Special Code List No.1 for traffic going to Minster and Ramsgate. Shunt and Trip movements are permitted towards both of the other two boxes on the Right Road, and Wrong Line moves are allowed to and from Archcliffe using the laid down codes for such movements.

All signals are colour lights and the subsidiaries are position light signals. The Outer Home and Home signals are two-aspect showing either red or yellow, as is now required for running signals at the approach to terminal stations, but all the others are three aspect except (for some unexplained reason) the starting signal from No.3 platform (No.72) which is two-aspect showing Red or Yellow. The Outer Home signal from Archcliffe has a route indicator giving the aspects M for the Main Road and 6 for No.6 Road. Similarly, the Inner Home (67/85/97) has a route indicator for three routes — 3, 4 and 5 Roads. The Home signal from Hawkesbury Street (17/18/31) also has a route indicator for the three platforms and Ferry Sidings. The Starting signals have route indicators as well for either the South Eastern road — A, or the Chatham line — F. The Inner Home from Archcliffe is situated very close to 61 crossover. Because this is so, the position light subsidiary at this signal (65) has to be operated for moves using these points towards the station.

Archcliffe Junction signal box seen from the northern corner of the triangle before the yard in the foreground was lifted. H.P. White

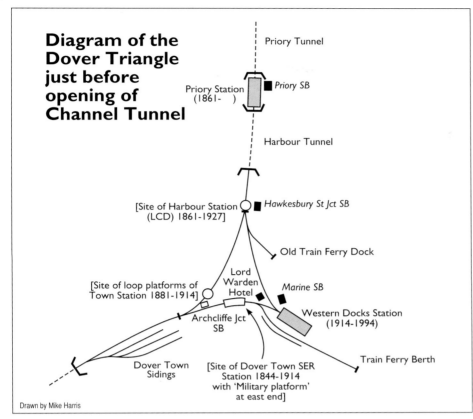

Diagram of the Dover Triangle just before opening of Channel Tunnel

Priory Tunnel

Priory Station (1861-)

Priory SB

Harbour Tunnel

[Site of Harbour Station (LCD) 1861-1927]

Hawkesbury St Jct SB

Old Train Ferry Dock

Lord Warden Hotel

[Site of loop platforms of Town Station 1881-1914]

Marine SB

Western Docks Station (1914-1994)

Archcliffe Jct SB

Train Ferry Berth

Dover Town Sidings

[Site of Dover Town SER Station 1844-1914 with 'Military platform' at east end]

Drawn by Mike Harris

There are four platforms numbered 3 to 6. Platforms 3 and 4 are normally reserved for Boat trains, platform 5 for the Dover Priory and Chatham traffic and platform 6 for loco hauled trains, such as the Inter City train from the north. With the inevitable rationalisation of the track work in recent years it is not now possible to run round a train by sending the locomotive beyond the station and bringing it back to the front of its train by routeing it round the outside of the station via what are now called the Ferry Sidings. Buffer stops have been placed at the end of each platform. The procedure is now as follows. A pilot loco is brought onto the end of the coaches and draws them back into the Dover Town Sidings through 74 points (the old Loco Shed turnout). The train engine being released, it follows the shunt move-

ment into these sidings. The pilot runs round in the sidings and hauls the carriages back into platform 6. The train engine follows and re-joins its train. The pilot is then trapped at the buffers until departure time. It used to be possible for the pilot to propel the carriages back into the platform but this was stopped because for a short while the driver of the pilot loco loses sight of the shunter during the propelling move. The line is sharply curved and a high wall blocks the driver's view. A barrier crossing controlled from the Box is situated on the Hawkesbury leg. These barriers are not lowered for incoming trains until Train Entering Section is received from Hawkesbury Street.

The levers working 17, 18 and 31 and 67, 85 and 97, the Home signals, also work the Draw Ahead signals placed at these posts. Each of

the platform roads has two track circuits. If the one nearest to the buffer stops only is occupied the Draw Ahead signal automatically comes off when any of the above levers are pulled. If, however, the Track Circuit at the end of the platform furthest from the buffer stops is occupied, then the Draw Ahead signal will not come off until a release button is pressed before pulling the appropriate lever.

Some of the signal locking is a little unusual. 73 shunt which controls moves from the old Loco Sidings leads 60 shunt situated at 108 points which lead to No.6 platform or the Train Ferry Sidings, but if the move is from the 73 shunt over 61 points to Nos.3 or 4 platforms then 82 shunt at 88 points has to be pulled before 73. The shunt signals at the platform ends must be pulled before the respective shunt signals ahead of them come off. So 53, 112, 38 and 110 lead 111 and 28, 89, 72 and 16 lead 80. All other cases where two or more signals have to be pulled for a particular route are operated backwards in the normally accepted practice.

A number of points have to be pulled before others can be worked. For example: 70 leads 11, 23 leads 34 which in turn leads 35 or 42.

A further peculiarity is that trains routed from Platform 6 or the Ferry Sidings to Hawkesbury Street cause the barriers on this leg of the triangle to be held down until they have cleared the Track Circuit beyond the level crossing. So, if Hawkesbury Street cannot get the train over its junction, then the Barrier Control lever — No.32 — is locked in the frame until the train has moved on, even though the barriers are themselves clear and the Track circuit covering them is also unoccupied. Trains leaving Platforms 4 and 5 do not cause this problem. It is usual, therefore, for the signalman to ascertain from the Hawkesbury Street signalman that he can get the train over his junction before letting it leave.

In the not-too-distant future all of these signal boxes, their interesting apparatus and methods of working will disappear as the new Ashford and Gillingham Signalling Centres come into being. That they have survived so long is a testimony to the thoroughness with which these frames, instruments, signals etc, were built. The railways cannot complain that they have not had their money's worth!

Class 47 diesel No.47422 enters Dover Priory with the 0618 Manchester Piccadilly to Folkestone Central in July 1989 on a service since withdrawn.
John Scrace

The Channel Tunnel and its Rail Access

Transport Consultant John Glover looks at the chequered history and vital need for an adequate London-Channel Tunnel rail link.

The idea of a Channel Tunnel had been discussed for nearly two centuries before the final decision to construct was taken in 1987. First suggested to Napoleon in 1802, the early plans came to nothing. This was partly because they were ahead of the practical engineering techniques of their day; and partly through fears (on the British side anyway) of invasion.

Such considerations continued to damn progress throughout most of the nineteenth century, though the technical feasibility gradually improved. It was Sir Edward Watkin who, as Chairman, persuaded the South Eastern Railway to begin experimental boring near Folkestone in 1881. This work too came to nought, but it is clear that

Watkin had wider designs. In his book 'Our Railways' of 1894, John Pendleton described the Parliamentary battle which surrounded the transformation of the Manchester, Sheffield and Lincolnshire Railway (of which Watkin was also Chairman) into its London Extension and the creation of the Great Central. It is worth quoting at length from one of the Bill Committee meetings.

Above **Though the rolling stock will differ, 'Eurostar' trains will be traversing this low-grade infrastructure for many years. In August 1979 a 4BEP (Buffet Car) unit heads for Dover through Sandling, now immediately west of the Dolland Moor Tunnel interchange sidings.**
John Glover

Mr Bidder, the QC for all the opponents in 1891, declared that the object of the Bill was not to serve the towns and villages on the route of the proposed new line, but to satisfy the ambitions of the promoters to become a great trunk line to London. It was, he said meaningly, to accomplish the deep laid ambitions of one man ... whose hope and dream was to terminate his life by running through carriages from the north to London, and from London to Paris. The Channel Tunnel was part and parcel of Sir Edward Watkins's dream, and he was now leading forward the shareholders of the Manchester, Sheffield and Lincolnshire Railway to ruin in the wild belief that this great line would increase their dividends.

As Watkin, himself a Manchester man, was also Chairman of the Metropolitan Railway, the South Eastern Railway and of what became the Channel Tunnel Company, Mr Bidder's accusations have a ring of truth. Alas, the Great Central largely met its end a quarter century or more ago, although it is interesting that its remains still attract entrepreneurial attention for the development of international rail traffic. However, the Channel Tunnel project progressed no further, since the Board of Trade at the insistence of the War Office ordered that work should cease.

The Watkin episode has been related at length, since it contains some worthwhile messages. First, a Channel Tunnel on its own is of little use to anybody other than those living near its portals. What is required additionally is wider access, whether only by rail as seems to have been assumed universally in the last century, or by a combination of road and rail as today. Traffic will be attracted by the size and extent of the business, consumer and tourist markets, and the leisure facilities and manufacturing industries that can be more easily reached. Access to the Channel Tunnel, then as now, is thus a key consideration. The more that a planned and unified approach can be taken (not necessarily under the control of a single individual!), the greater the potential value to its owners in particular and to the nation as a whole.

There was then a lull until the late 1920s, when a Royal Commission was set up. Electric traction was now thoroughly feasible; remarkably, Watkin had proposed steam! However, a House of Commons debate on 30th June 1930 put paid to the idea for the foreseeable future. Nevertheless, the Southern Railway was determined to improve its Continental connections, and 1929 saw the inauguration of the *Golden Arrow* from London to Dover and the luxury steamer *Canterbury* thence across the Channel. Paris was reached 6hrs 35mins after departure from Victoria. Matters did not stop there either, for in 1936 the completion of train ferry berths at Dover and Dunkirk, with new ships to suit, enabled the establishment of through rail facilities to France. Passengers were offered the *Night Ferry* with its Wagon-Lits sleeping cars for through London-Paris travel.

With the onset of World War II, Continental services were decidedly in abeyance, and it was 1957 before the Channel Tunnel idea emerged again. Or, rather, a fixed Channel Link, since by then what was on offer was the choice between a rail tunnel, a rail and road tunnel, and a bridge (for either or both). The debate continued for many years, with the addition of a scheme postu-

lating road bridges at both ends and a tunnel in the centre section. And should tunnel schemes use immersed tubes or be bored? Evaluation considered cost, technical feasibility, the navigational implications (of a bridge) and the ventilation implications (of a tunnel). A rail only tunnel was consistently shown to be superior.

Political interest was rising, to the extent that the 1968 Transport Act provided for the establishment of a Channel Tunnel Planning Council, charged with the job of sorting out the operational requirements, planning the financial arrangements, and generally getting all ready. But the time was not yet ripe, and the 1974 fiasco when work was actually started and then abandoned was a severe blow.

Yet the reasons for abandonment were as much to do with access to the tunnel as the affordability of the tunnel construction costs. Total passenger traffic between London and Paris was growing fast, rising from 1.0m to 1.5m a year between 1960 and 1970. Furthermore this was major growth by air transport at the expense of slowly declining surface modes. In 1971, British Rail was expecting the tunnel to double rail passenger carryings by the time it was opened (in 1978!), representing roundly two-thirds of the rapidly expanding market. Similarly robust conclusions were made for freight traffic.

What chance, then, of carrying the additional traffic on the existing railway? Leaving aside the problem of the British loading gauge, which does not permit the passage of standard Continental rail vehicles, the existing routes have finite capacity, much of which is effectively dedicated to London commuter traffic. The 1970s conclusion was that a new rail link was inevitable. The route would have large radius curves and be capable of taking trains with very high speeds for most of its length. The ruling gradient would be 1 in 70. It was also correspondingly costly, while the furore in the Kent and Surrey commuter belt was immense and implacable. In retrospect, neither the practical nor the financial implications of extensive new construction were thought through sufficiently.

However, the project did not go away, the next port of call being a cheap single-track rail tunnel. This would have carried conventional rail traffic only, without any facility for a car and heavy goods vehicle shuttle. It would have been constructed to Continental loading gauge, and its capacity was put at 60 trains a day in each direction. London-Paris was billed at a 4hr 30min journey time. The scheme found no favour.

And so we reached the Channel Tunnel Act 1987, and the establishment of Eurotunnel and the construction company Trans Manche Link (TML). A large proportion of the traffic will consist of 'Le Shuttle' services between Cheriton and Fréthun. In Britain, such traffic will then take to the roads. Through rail passengers will be offered the newly designed 'Eurostar' services between Waterloo and Paris (in 3hr 0min) or Brussels. Longer distance services in Britain and overnight services will come later.

The physical limitations of the established boat train routes to London, although benefiting from considerable investment generally and access to a new terminal at Waterloo International, still exist. In two hours from leaving London by InterCity, one can be in York, Crewe, Cardiff or Exeter. All of these are in the 145-190 mile bracket. It

takes the same time to get to Ramsgate, a mere 80 miles. It is journey time rather than maximum speed which is important. Nevertheless, that also means that on high speed lines stopping must be infrequent. No fewer than 17 new and preferably international stations in the c70 miles from the proposed Kings Cross terminal to Cheriton have been proposed by hopeful communities.

There are three objectives for the new rail link:
(1) To provide the main rail link between Britain and Continental Europe.
(2) To provide a major increase in both route capacity and quality of journeys between Kent and London (a benefit to both commuters and businesses).
(3) To provide the transport spine for the East Thames Corridor development, helping to shift development pressures from the west to the east of London.

As things stand, there are going to be capacity constraints. The ceiling for Waterloo International et al is put at 25 million passengers per year, and this level will be reached in the first decade of the next century. The implication is that within a few years a further 20 million journeys would have to be made by other means. This is bad business for the railways, let alone the economic and environmental implications.

The CTRL also offers London–Cheriton in 38 minutes (compare with the present 78 minutes in the evening peak from Waterloo), while sample NSE times from Ashford to London would be 37 minutes, from the Medway Towns 23 minutes, and Dartford 17 minutes. Broadly, these represent a halving of journey times, and a 50% increase in capacity. Similar gains are to be had in the East Thames area, but in all cases there is a need to integrate with the existing railway infrastructure and identify the scope for exploiting the development gains.

Productive transport investment is essential if Britain is to compete in Europe in the first quarter of the next century. High speed railways improve accessibility between whole regions, bringing economic benefits in their broadest sense. King's Cross, together with St Pancras and Euston, forms the focus for InterCity's services. The new St Pancras International station, with its 138 acres for development, will become the world's first hub and spoke railport, feeding passengers into and out of the existing network.

As a world class city in its own right, London must be careful not to undersell itself. It is the prime financial and business centre in Europe, international communications are superb, it has a fortunate geographical position, and in many ways good infrastructure. But it is under competition from Frankfurt, and perhaps Paris. The construction of CTRL would bring some indirect gains. These are put at being worth up to £1bn, and result from the benefits to international travellers which accrue to London as such, rather than rail operators through the farebox.

A new rail link is much more than just a commercial venture. Perhaps the issue of greatest importance is the breadth of vision which will be encompassed. Above all it should be a railway for the future, carrying freight and passenger traffic on a high quality alignment with minimal environmental problems. Freight, in full size continental freight wagons and all forms of combined transport, should be able to access at least as far as London.

Professor H.P. White, Pat to those who knew him, died on 21st February 1994 as this Album was being finalised. He had been the Editor of RSE since 1991.

Pat had always a passion for railways and his career started as booking clerk at Charlton Station. War service saw him in the Royal Artillery in the Far East and subsequent capture at the fall of Singapore. During four years incarceration in a PoW camp in Formosa he kept his sanity by planning imaginary trips over the British railway network. These plans were later put into practice and provided much information for later railway articles. After the War and a period of recuperation, Pat enrolled at Queen Mary's College London under the government education scheme for demobbed servicemen. Here he gained the Top First for his year and went on to do his MA. His first lecturing post was at Edinburgh University. In 1952 he went to the University of West Africa and travelled the Gold Coast, Sierra Leone and Nigeria where he taught many people, some of whom became their country's leaders.

In 1963 he took the post of tutor attached to the Arts Department of the College of Advanced Technology in Salford, near Manchester. Salford soon became one of the new generation of universities and over the next 20 years he established the geography department. A leader in transport economics, he was appointed Professor in 1972. In 1982 tired of battling with education cuts he took early retirement and moved to Godmanchester near Huntingdon.

Although retired he did more work than ever. Apart from writing and updating Regional Railway Histories of Southern England and Greater London and Forgotten Railways he was editor of the Railway and Canal Historical Society Journal and Past President of that Society. He even found time to be a booking clerk on the Nene Valley Railway, going back to the start of his career. He was also a Lay Preacher for the Godmanchester Church. Occasionally he took services at other churches and I remember once at Brampton the organist playing one of the railway themes as we entered.

Always willing to help in transport and other matters, I knew him not only as an author but as a friend.

Allan Mott